MASTERING TINKERCAD

INSTRUCTOR

ED CHARLWOOD

PUBLISHED BY

1st Edition April 2024

ISBN-13: 979-8-9881894-2-8 (Student Version)

ISBN-13: 979-8-9881894-3-5 (Instructor Version)

Library of Congress Control Number: ##########

Publisher: CADclass

Written By: Edward Charlwood

Edited: Jake O Sugden & Joshua Manley

Saturn Apollo Program: NASA ID: 6401974 was photographed by NASA. This file is in the public domain in the United States because it was solely created by NASA. (https://images.nasa.gov/details/6401974).
House numeric labels. Created by Cmdrjameson and is licensed under CC BY-SA 3.0 DEED Attribution-ShareAlike 3.0 Unported. (https://commons.wikimedia.org/wiki/File:House_numeric_labels.PNG)
"Telephone Classic" CAD Tinkercad model by ZDP189 and is licensed under CC BY-SA 3.0 DEED Attribution-ShareAlike 3.0 Unported. (https://www.tinkercad.com/things/4OJJ8aSqYrz-telephone-classic).

For information on distribution, translation, or bulk sales, contact Ed@CADclass.org directly.

About the Authors

Ed Charlwood is an award-winning educator and expert in CAD curricula development, with a Bachelor's degree in Engineering & Product Design and a Master's in Education from Cambridge University.

With 20 years of teaching experience and a passion for empowering students, Ed has crafted STEM curricula for 10,000+ students worldwide.

His approach to teaching has earned him prestigious accolades and recognition, including the honor of being a Google Certified Innovator, an Apple Distinguished Educator, and an Autodesk Academic Partner. He also serves as a Fellow of the Royal Society, which recognizes people who make a "substantial contribution to the improvement of natural knowledge, including mathematics, engineering science, and medical science." He's a member of the Tinkercad Instructor Advisory Board.

Professor Joshua Manley is an entrepreneur and educator with a passion for making. He is a published scientist who ran a science tutoring business in New York City, teaching Math, Chemistry, Biology, Physics, and SAT/ACT prep. He then led the education department of one of the nation's largest and most successful makerspaces. He's taught thousands of students, educators, and administrators worldwide. His TED-Ed talk about bicycle physics has millions of views.

Jake O Sugden is a mechanical engineer and lifelong maker passionate about engineering and design. He taught many making disciplines at one of the nation's premier makerspaces, testing many of the concepts found in this book over the last six years with thousands of students. He is co-owner of CADclass, an CAD education company focused on product development and education. He's an Autodesk expert who works with these programs daily.

How To Use This Book

Welcome to the fantastic world of Tinkercad!

Get ready to mix fun and learning and pick up some amazing new design skills.

This workbook is your trusty sidekick to the tutorials waiting for you at **Tinkercad.com/learn**. So jump in, then come back here to test your skills, push your limits, and take on exciting challenges. Let the adventure begin!

To keep track of your progress, you should check these boxes.

If you see one of these, write your answer in it. 

There is a glossary at the back. Write definitions on the dashed lines as you find them out.

When you see this .... write your answer on it.

Pan ...Changes the view left/right or up/down

The most important thing is to play, explore, and have fun.

If you'd like to read this on a computer or iPad, visit CADclass.org/pages/books for a free or donation-based copy of this book and others.

How To Use This Book 

Welcome to the fantastic world of Tinkercad! We are delighted that you are empowering your students with this fantastic tool.

- This workbook is designed to accompany the excellent tutorials at **Tinkercad.com/learn**
- You will need to sign up and create a Tinkercad Class beforehand: **t.ly/PUzHV**
- Join our Discord server to collaborate and share ideas: **discord.gg/5hbt6xDPqf**

All the pages with a grey background like this one are for teachers and instructors. They provide answers, links, QR codes for further reading, and valuable background knowledge to add depth and richness to your students' stories.

The student workbook is divided into colored sections representing tools, techniques, and program functionality. They can use the checkboxes to keep track of progress, answer questions in circles, and even write longer answers on dashed lines.

There are many open-ended challenges for your students to attempt. These help expand their knowledge and reinforce learning. There is specific vocabulary used in CAD, and students must develop fluency in using it. Students can add definitions to the glossary at the back as they go along.

You will also notice that students are sometimes asked to match icons to tools they haven't used. This is deliberate. Research shows that if students attempt answers they don't know, they will retain information better when they learn it later. This book is carefully sequenced in a logical, interleaved way. We suggest your students follow along to build their knowledge, skills, and understanding.

Most importantly, have fun, learn, encourage exploration... and enjoy!

What is CAD?

Imagine you're an architect and you want to build an amazing skyscraper. You wouldn't just start stacking bricks, right?

CAD stands for Computer-Aided Design. It's a type of software that helps you create robots, buildings, cars, or anything else you can think of, on a computer.

Using CAD, you can test out ideas, like changing the shape of a building or modeling a new rocket shape. You can even simulate how things will work, like seeing if a car's engine will fit under the hood.

Once you're happy with your design, you can send it to a 3D printer or a laser cutter.

Designers and Engineers are human superheroes with unique skills to improve the world. They created everything you see, hear, touch, and feel.

CAD is like having a superpower that lets you design and create anything you can imagine. So, let's master Tinkercad, a powerful tool that real architects, engineers, and designers use daily to bring their ideas to life.

What is CAD? 

The acronym CAD stands for Computer-Aided Design, which involves using a computer to help you design digital items.

Before CAD, 3D models and engineering drawings were all created by hand using pencils, erasers, T-squares, and set squares. Even after all the manual labor, the engineers and toolmakers had to start from scratch and make the sketches all over again if a change was required.

It looked like this:

NASA designers in the 1960s
t.ly/PObce

The first 747 "jumbo jet" flown in 1969 was designed using 75,000 paper drawings of 4.5 million parts, 136 miles of electrical wiring, 5 landing gear legs, 4 hydraulic systems, and 10 million labor hours. Read more via the QR code:

Many CAD designs are linked to CAM (Computer-Aided Manufacturing).

50 years ago, the first 747 took off
t.ly/nbBDk

CAD is always evolving to increase speed/power, access, & collaboration. We're already seeing examples of AI-powered modeling.

Everyday examples of CAD could include:

- Microsoft Powerpoint / Google Slides.
- Adobe Photoshop to create graphic designs
- Music software like MuseScore, Sibelius or GarageBand.
- Python or Swift Playgrounds to create code
- Minecraft to create 3D virtual worlds

Do Now: Student ▶

If you are in a school:

1. Go to Tinkercad.com

2. Click **Login** in the top right corner

3. Select **Students with Class Code**

4. Enter the code your Instructor gave you and press **Go to my class**

5. Click **Create** then **3D Design**

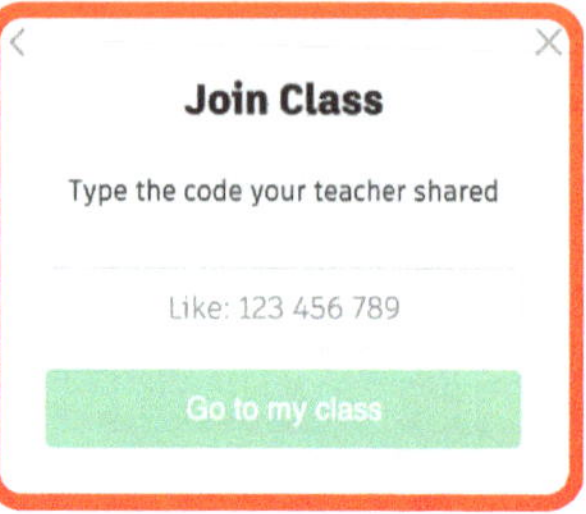

If you are on your own:

1. Go to Tinkercad.com

2. Click **Sign Up** in the top right

3. Select **Create a personal account**

4. Create an account using one of the options

5. Click **Create** then **3D Design**

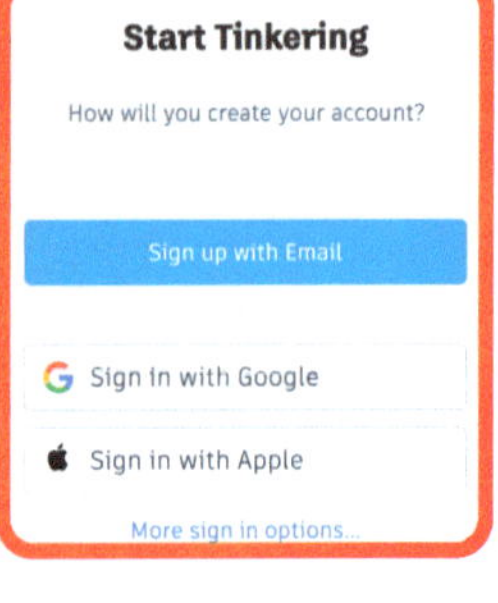

Do Now: Instructor 

If you are a instructor.

1. Go to **Tinkercad.com**

2. Click **Sign Up** in the top right corner.

3. Read the overview, then select **Continue to start making my educator account.**

4. Read the terms. If you agree, select **I agree.**

5. Navigate to the **Classes** tab on the left-hand side of the dashboard.

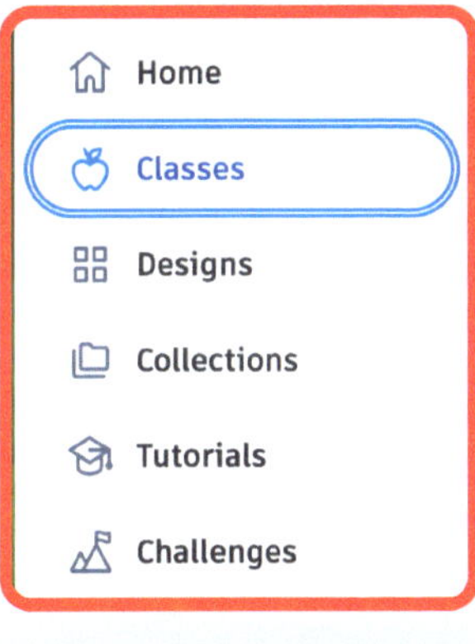

6. Select **Create new class.**

7. Follow the detailed instructions here to get your classes, co-instructors, and activities prepared t.ly/PUzHV

8. You will need students to access the Gallery, so you must turn off **Safe Mode**.

9. Join the CADclass Discord to collaborate and share ideas: discord.gg/5hbt6xDPqf

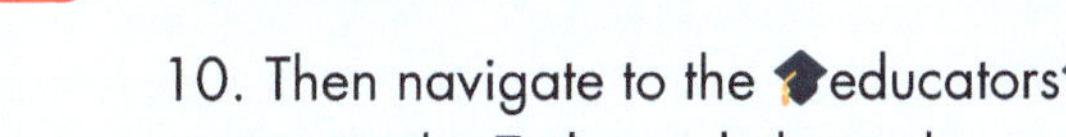

10. Then navigate to the 🎓educators🎓 section in the Tinkercad channel.

Dashboard

The Tinkercad icon gets you back to the dashboard.

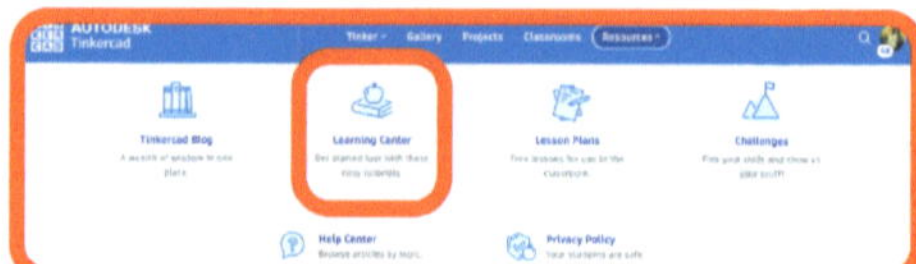

Access the Learning Center and Challenges via Resources.

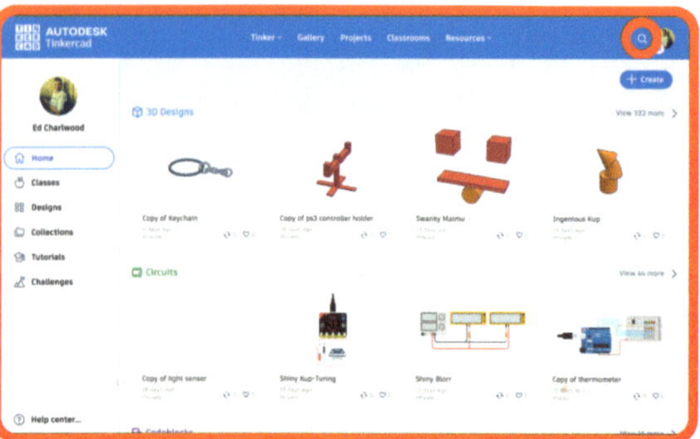

You can also access the Gallery of public designs here.

This page is your Dashboard. Press the Tinkercad icon in the top left to get back to it.

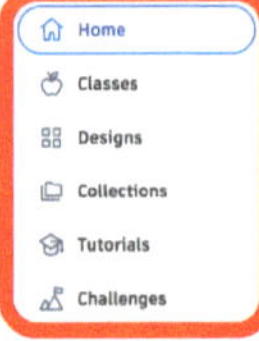

Use the buttons on the left to access your Classes, Designs, Collections and more.

Your designs

DO NOW

To create a new 3D Design press **+ Create** and then **3D Design** to open a 3D Workspace.

Dashboard

Access or delete your recent designs using this button.

Fantastic Gogo-Sango

This page is your 3D design workspace.

The Workplane is the blue grid in the middle.

The searchable library of pre-made shapes is on the right.

UI: Mouse 

If you have a 3-button mouse, we recommend using it for Tinkercad for navigating the UI (User Interface).

Left click on the purple Cone and drag it onto the blue Workplane.

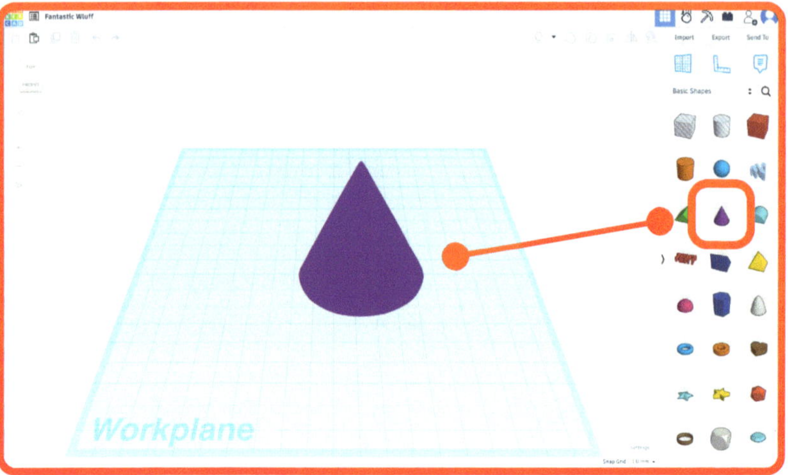

Next up, right-click and move the mouse. Did it **rotate** or **zoom in**?

....

Hold the mouse wheel and drag the mouse side to side. Does this **zoom out** or **pan** side-to-side?

....

UI: Touchpad 

The touchpad is an alternative to the mouse and is found in the center of your laptop, below your keyboard. They all work differently so you may need to experiment to figure it out.

Click on the purple cone and drag it onto the blue Workplane.

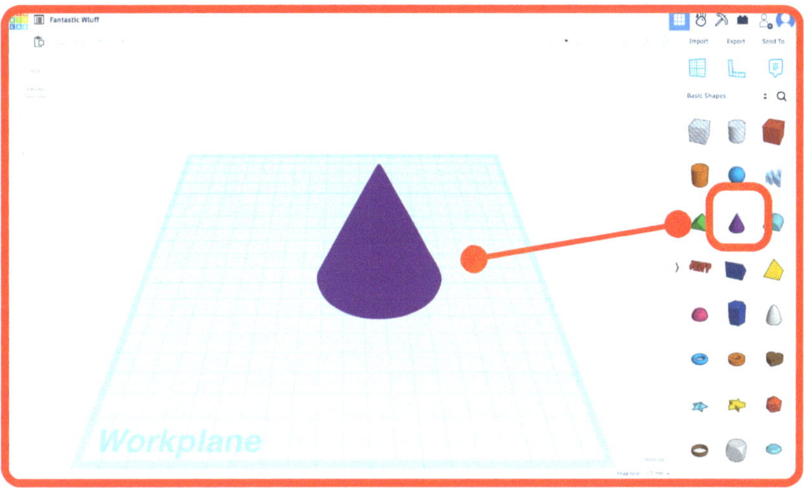

Touch the touchpad with 2 fingers and pinch in. Did it **rotate** or **zoom out**?

....

Press and hold with 2 fingers and move side to side. Does this **zoom out** or **orbit** around?

....

Drag the purple Cone onto the blue Workplane.

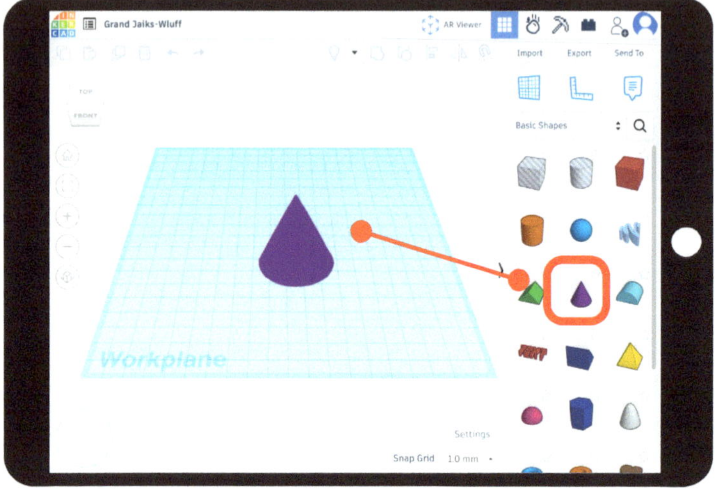

Tap the screen with 2 fingers and pinch closed. Did it **rotate** or **zoom out**?

....

Press and move side to side with 2 fingers. Does this **zoom out** or **pan** side-to-side?

....

New Design 

Congratulations, the cone in the workspace is your first 3D Design!

Whenever you see this box, you need to save your work and start a new 3D Design.

Save it
Name it "CADclass 1"

1. Click in the name box in the top-left.

2. Type in "CADclass 1" and press enter on the keyboard.

3. Click the Tinkercad logo in the top left to return to the dashboard.

4. Start a new 3D Design.

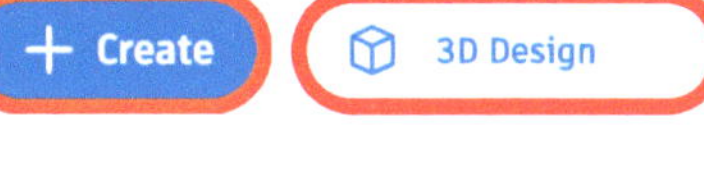

Solutions 

First up, what happens if you left-click and drag a Cone?

A: The left mouse button selects shape/function (click) or moves a shape [click > hold > drag]

Next up, right-click and move the mouse. Did it **rotate** or **zoom in**?

A: The RIGHT button rotates the view [click > hold > drag]

Hold the mouse wheel and drag the mouse side to side. Does this **zoom out** or **pan**?

A: The mouse wheel zooms in/out when rolled, and also pans side-to-side [click > hold > drag + move]

Tap the screen with 2 fingers and pinch closed. Did it **rotate** or **zoom out**?

A: The pinch together motion typically zooms out, while pinch open zooms in.

Press and move side to side with 2 fingers. Does this **zoom out** or **pan** side-to-side?

A: 2 fingers pans side-to-side.

UI: iPad

Tap the screen with 2 fingers and pinch closed. Did it **rotate** or **zoom out**?

A: Out

Press and move side to side with 2 fingers. Does this **zoom out** or **pan** side-to-side? 

A: Pan

Place It

Welcome to Tinkercad, where creative projects start by placing simple shapes!

Click and drag the red Box from the library on the right-hand side onto the blue Workplane.

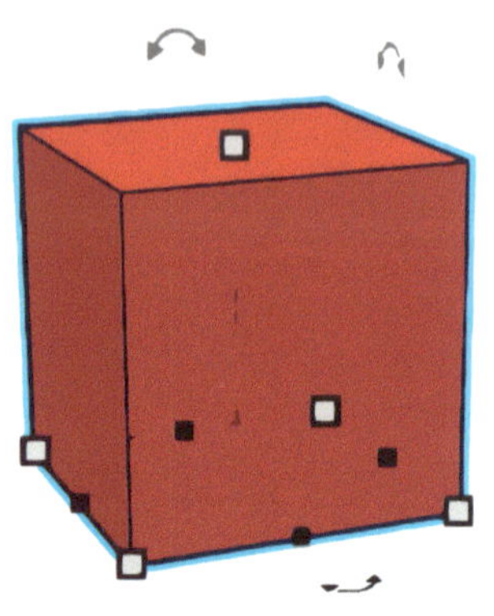

Click and drag the **White Boxes** surrounding the cube. What happened!?!

....

But wait, there's more! Hold down the Shift key, then click, hold, and drag those same White Boxes. What was different?

....

Ready for the next trick... click, hold and drag **Black Squares.** Tell me what *that* did:

....

One more thing! Click, hold and drag the **Black Cone.** What directions did the cube go?

....

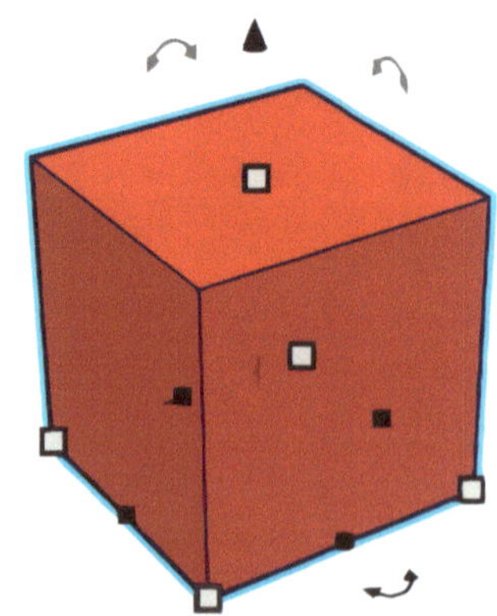

Place It

Did you catch that surprise when you clicked on a shape? A special box popped up called the Dialogue Box, filled with buttons, icons and sliders! Time to play around, transforming those shapes by pushing, pulling, and stretching.

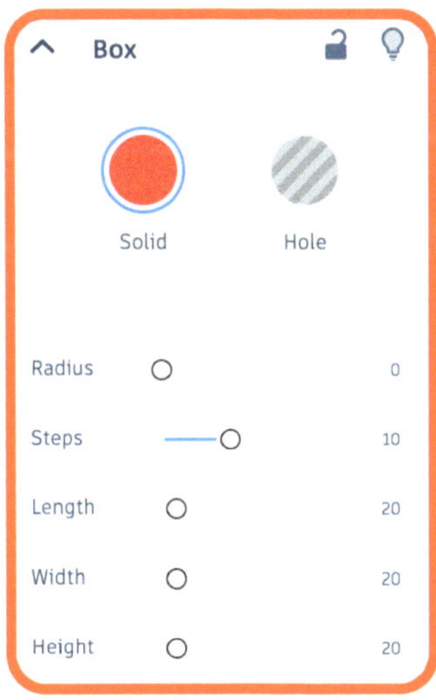

PLAY

With the same red Box selected click, hold and drag the sliders in the Dialogue Box.

You can also type numbers into the boxes on the right! Let's make a quick smartphone:

Radius: 1.0 mm
Steps: 5
Length: 147.6 mm
Width: 71.6 mm
Height: 7.8 mm

DO NOW

Save your work and start a new 3D Design following the steps on the New Design page.

Save it
Name it "CADclass Phone"

Place It 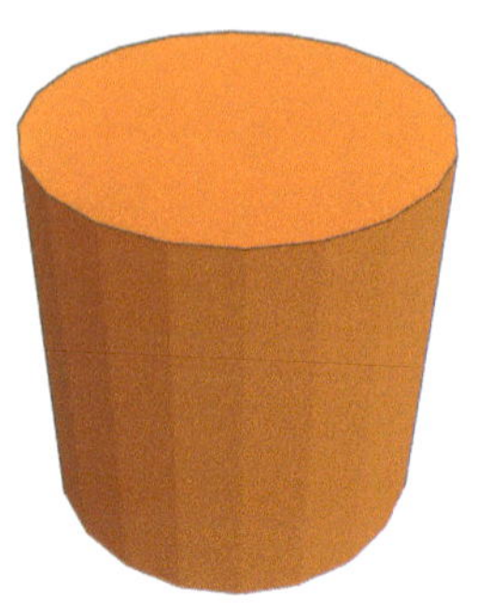

PLAY

Start a new 3D Design. Click and drag in an orange Cylinder. **Zoom In** using the mouse scroll wheel or pinching open, and take a close look!

But there are more tricks to explore! Let's go Cruising using Cruise mode. This feature lets you slide shapes onto other shapes and attach them as if they were magnetic.

PLAY

Press, hold, and drag the purple Cone onto the orange Cylinder but don't let go.

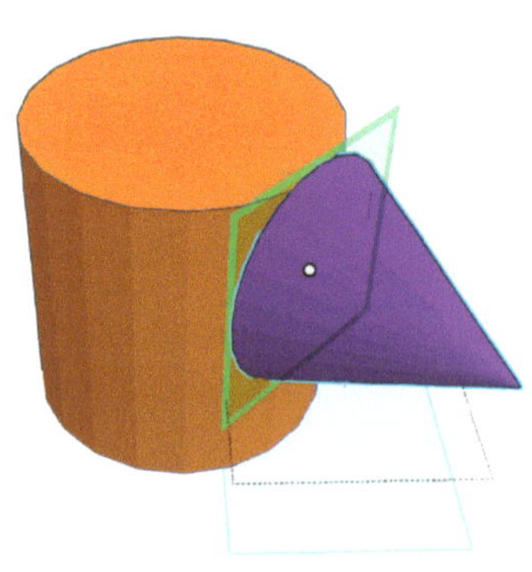

Move the Cone around the Cylinder and notice how it stays attached!

This is Cruise mode.

 Release the mouse to place it. To re-activate cruise mode, click the shape, press C or the Cruise icon, and drag the white dot.

Place It 📍

DO NOW

Save your work and start a new 3D Design following the steps on the New Design page.

Save it
Name it "CADclass Cruise"

Match the Icon + Word

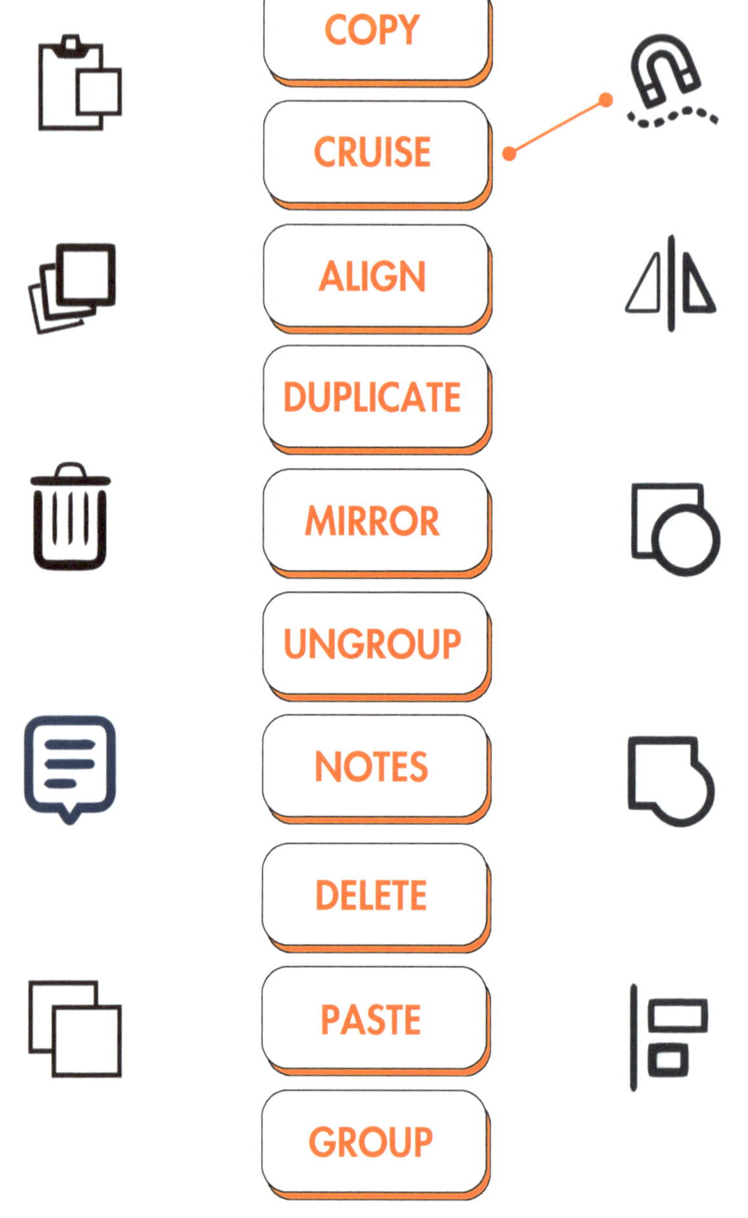

Solutions 

You will notice that students are asked to match icons to tools they have not yet used. This is deliberate.

Research shows that if students attempt answers they don't know, when they do learn it, they remember better.

Getting It Wrong: Surprising Tips on How to Learn
https://t.ly/frkm2

Solutions 

The white boxes are "handles" that allow you to resize shapes in 2 directions simultaneously.

Holding **Shift** is called an **Action Modifier** and will scale the 2 sides proportionally.

The black "handles" allows you to resize 1 direction at a time. The black "cone" allows you to move the shape above, through, or below the Workplane.

The sliders in the dialogue box change the value related to it. You can also type a value into the number box by clicking it.

The **Lock**, **Show/Hide**, **Solid,** and **Hole** icons appear in all dialogue boxes.

Shortcut "D" drops the shape back onto the Workplane.

Shortcuts in CAD enhance efficiency by allowing quick access to commands, saving time, improving precision, reducing mouse dependency, and facilitating multitasking.

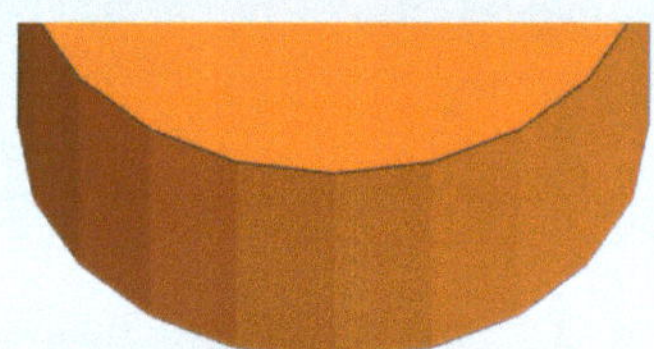

CAD programs often represent smooth surfaces using polygons for practical and computational reasons. While the surfaces in a CAD model may appear smooth to the human eye, they are actually made up of a mesh of polygons.

Calculating the geometry and shading of smooth surfaces is computationally expensive. Using polygons provides a simpler and more efficient way to represent and render the surface, allowing Tinkercad to run smoothly in a browser.

Solutions 

Cruise (or Cruising) is a feature that allows you to easily stack shapes on top of other shapes.

When you add a new shape Cruise is turned on by default.

Once you place the new shape a green "Shape Workplane helper" appears to help you move, rotate, or scale it in-place.

This vanishes when you make a new selection or use a new tool.

In **Cruise** mode, press Shift to flip the shape under the surface and make it a hole to cut it out.

To re-activate **Cruise**, select the shape, click **C**, then click-drag the white circle.

The **Scribble** tool is not used in the tower challenge because it opens a different interface and requires user design input.

But don't worry, you will explore Scribble later in the book.

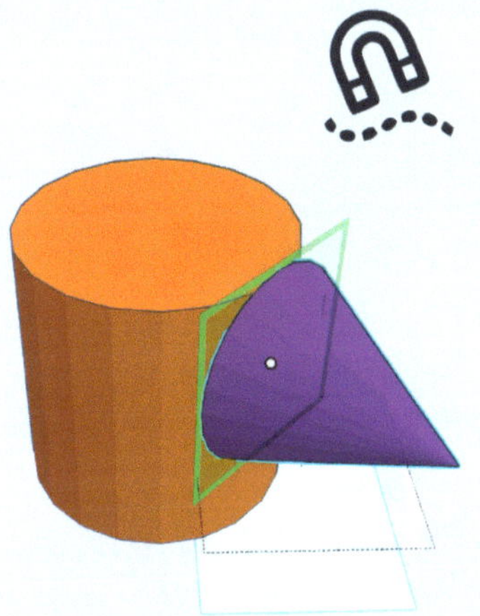

Re/activate **Cruise** by pressing keyboard shortcut "**C**."

Number the Features

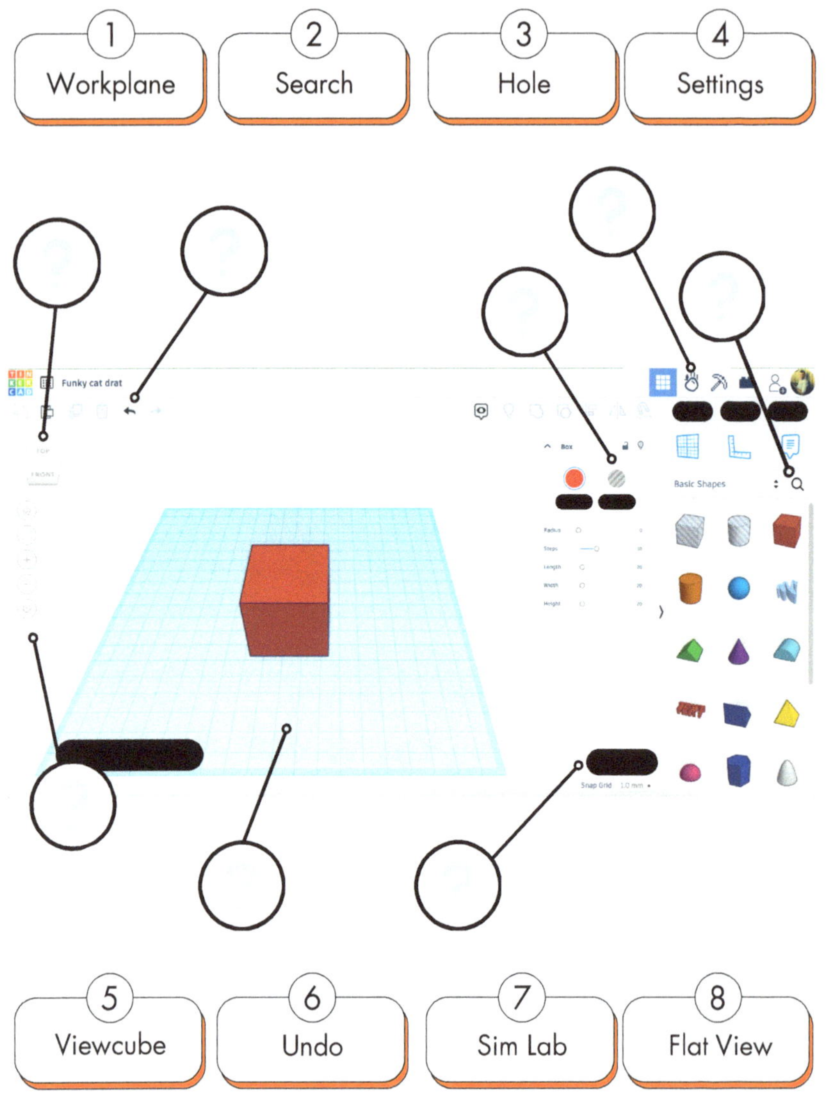

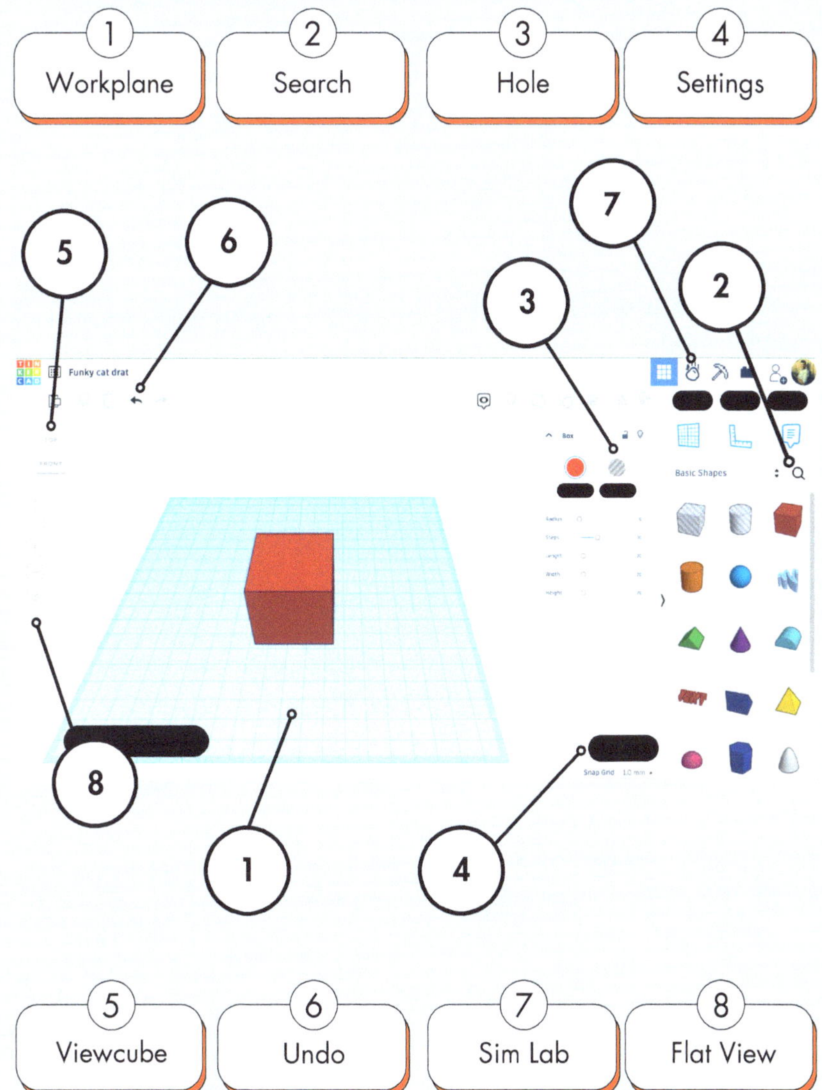

1 Workplane	2 Search	3 Hole	4 Settings

5 Viewcube	6 Undo	7 Sim Lab	8 Flat View

Move It »»»

Moving shapes onto and around the Workplane is a key skill. It's like setting up a board game and then moving the pieces with confidence. You can Move with your mouse, trackpad, and keyboard.

DO NOW

From the Dashboard, search the gallery using the 🔍 in the top right corner for *"CADclass Compass"*. Press **Copy and Tinker** to open it.

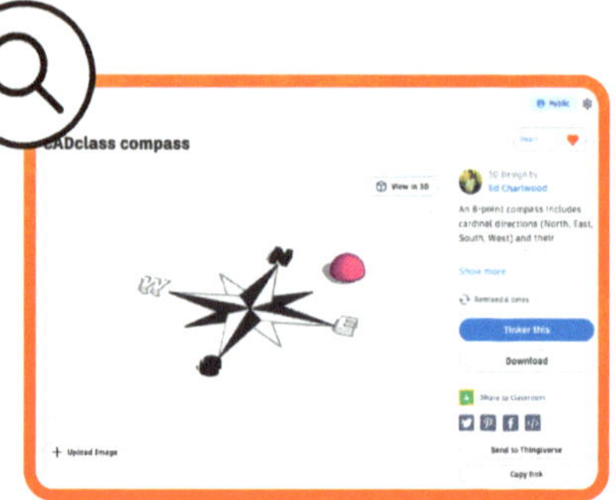

Copy and Tinker

You may see a message that says you can only see Staff Picks. This is because your class is in Safe Mode. Could you ask your instructor to change the setting on your Tinkercad Class page?

PLAY

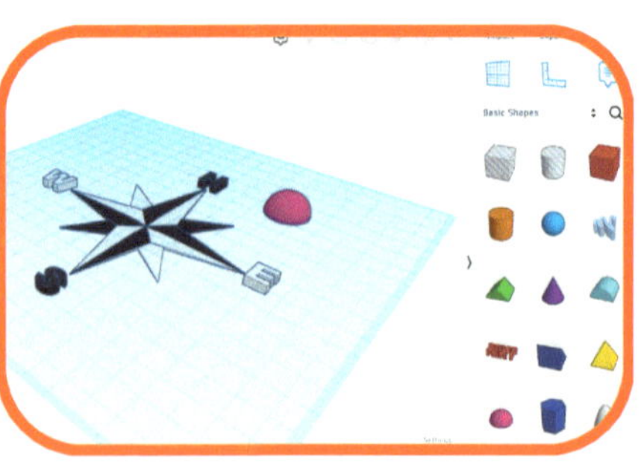

Place the pink half Sphere to cover East [E]. Click and drag it to cover North [N]. What are the coordinates in mm shown on screen? e.g. 0.0 , 0.0 mm

....

Move It ⟫⟫⟫

PLAY

While moving shapes with the mouse, hold down the Shift key. What happens?

....

Shapes can be moved using the arrow keys on your keyboard. To adjust the distance of movement, modify the **Snap Grid** below the **Settings** button.

Settings	
Snap Grid	5.0 mm ▲

Q: Can shapes be moved in 2 or 3 dimensions? Write your answer in the circle.

Save it
Name it "Compass"

2

CHALLENGE

What is the fewest arrow key presses can you move the pink Half Sphere in to cover? N > E > S > W ?

Solutions 

The compass challenge is designed to help students master different combinations of **Move** controls (including using the keyboard) and also to access, inspect, and use existing designs from the Gallery.

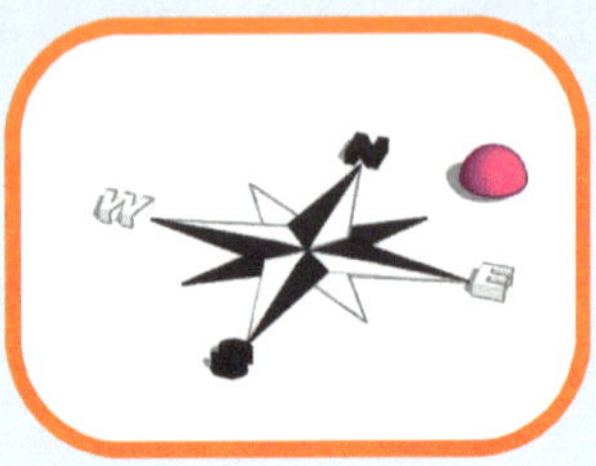

To use a design from the gallery you may have to press **Copy and Tinker**.

Copy and Tinker

You can react to designs, showing your appreciation to the designer.

The search page also shows useful information about the history of the design: when it was made, when it was edited, and if it is a remix of another design. It's helpful to check the provenance of a design.

This is a remix of **Compass** by **avram1912**.

The X and Y axes and also Z using the black cone icon (see Place It)

3

Students can move shapes using the keyboard arrow keys and change how much they move by changing the **Snap Grid** via the Settings button. The larger the grid, the fewer clicks to move.

A: If you press Shift while moving objects with the mouse, they will only move horizontally and vertically, not diagonally.

A: The coordinates from E to N are -57,-57.

2

Move It »»»

Let's quickly talk about 2D and 3D: 2D flat shapes only have length and width, no thickness. 3D shapes have 3 dimensions: length, width, and thickness.

DO NOW

From the Dashboard, search the Gallery 🔍 for "CADclass XYZ axis" and press **Copy and Tinker**.

Copy and Tinker

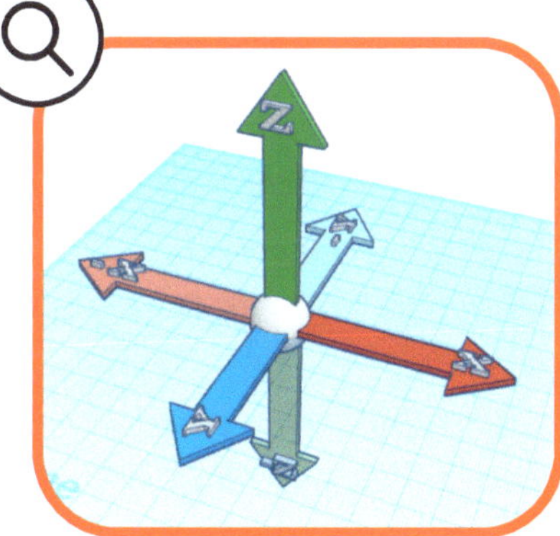

Move It >>>

PLAY

Practice moving the whole group in the X and Y axes using both of these:

1. Keyboard arrow keys
2. Mouse + Shift

The black cone lets you move shapes in the Z axis: above, below, or through the Workplane. Practice moving in the Z axis using:

3. The black cone

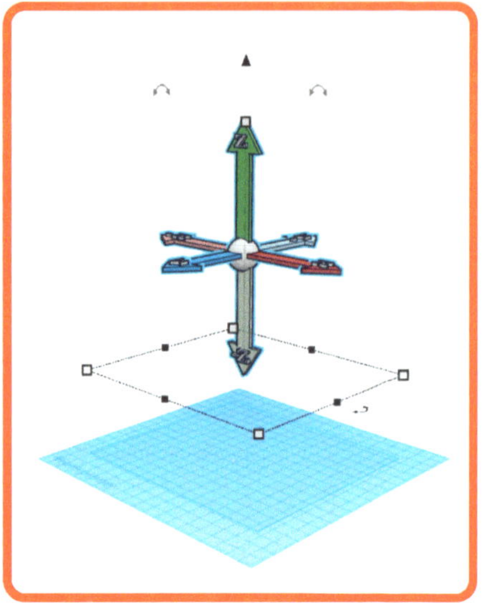

PLAY

Try the **Undo** and **Redo** actions.

Press Ctrl+Z to **Undo** an action and Ctrl+Y to **Redo** it.

There are also **Undo** and **Redo** buttons in the top left.

PLAY

Press **D** on the keyboard to "**Drop**" a part moved from the Workplane back onto to the Workplane.

Save it
Name it "[your name] XYZ Axis"

Solutions 

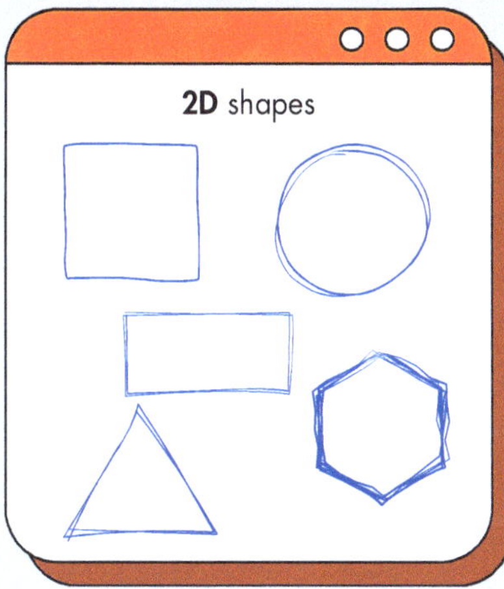

2D shapes

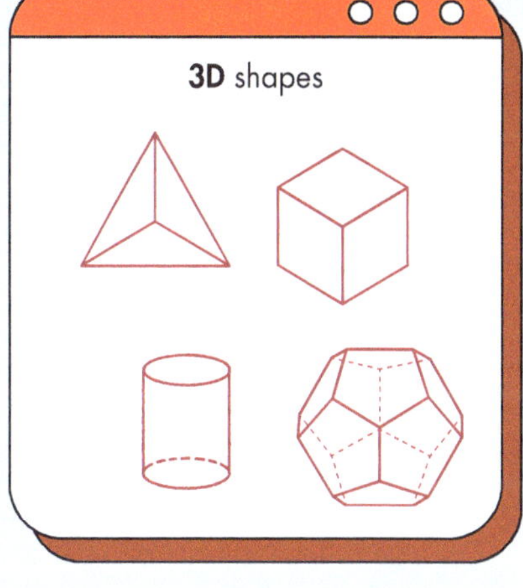

3D shapes

2D shapes include squares, triangles, rectangles, circles, polygons (hexagon, pentagon, etc), and more.

3D shapes include the Platonic solids, such as the tetrahedron, a pyramid with a triangular base, and three triangular faces meeting at a common vertex.

YOU COULD

- Make links to other subjects e.g. Geography (map reading), Maths (graphing).
- Look at other CAD software like Autodesk Fusion and Onshape and note how 3 axes are used
- Use this language with CAM, like preparing a file for 3D printing.
- Use fingers to point in 2 axes (make an L shape with the thumb and index finger) and 3 axes
https://t.ly/YOs53

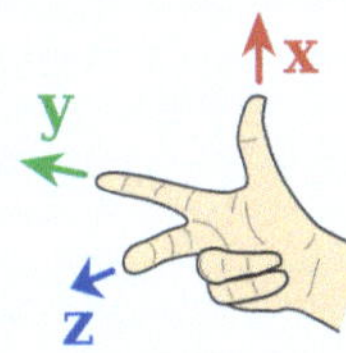

VIDEO

Overview of 3D Printing
t.ly/bpX8c

View It 👓

DO NOW

Search and add the "Printable Dice" from the Shapes Library.

Q: Two numbers are missing from the Dice. Write the total here:

PLAY

Click on a shape. Find the lightbulb icon in the Dialogue Box. Press it. What just happened?

3

CHALLENGE

Add the missing numbers to the Dice using the Text tool.

....

Bring it back using:
Ctrl + Shift + H or the press drop-down menu next to the lightbulb icon.

View It 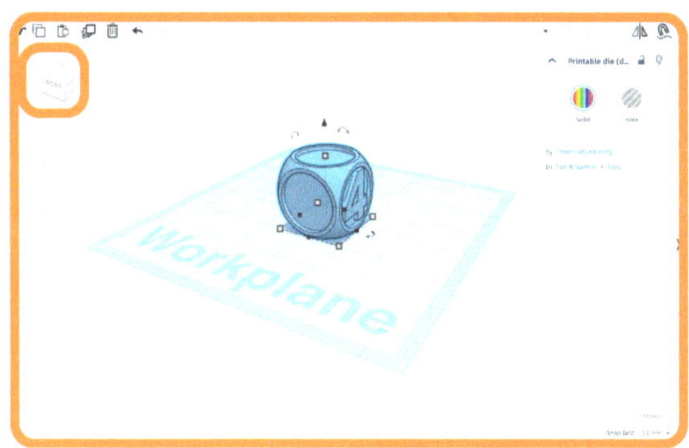

The Viewcube is navigation tool. You can move it and the Workplane moves, or, you can move the Workplane and the Viewcube moves. It has clickable faces, edges and vertices (corners).

PLAY

Click the Right face.

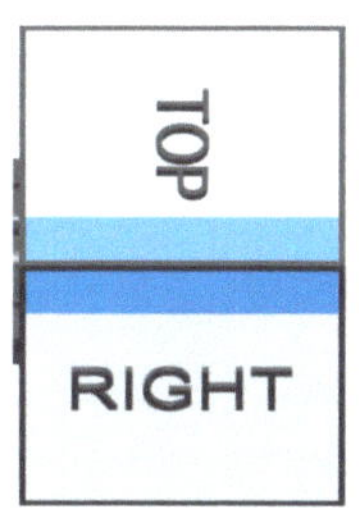

Click the Top/Right edge.

Click the Top / Front/Right vertex.

Q: Add up the number of edges, faces, and vertices a cube has and write it here

View It 👓

Sometimes its better not to use your mouse to navigate around your 3D model. The View Buttons on the lefthand side of the screen are handy shortcuts.

Click each one of the View Buttons and describe what each does.

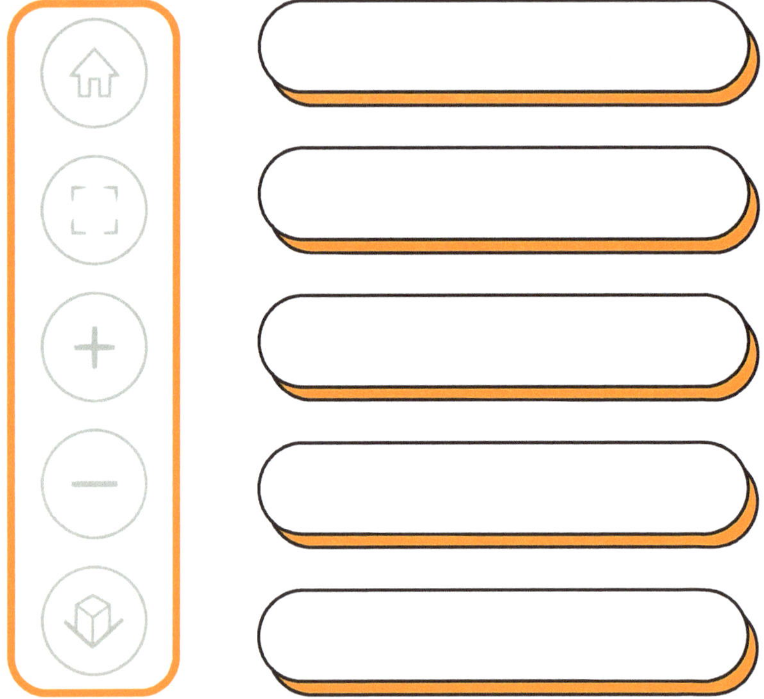

Name it "[your name] Printable Dice"

Press the recent designs button, then select New Design.

Solutions 

You don't have to restrict yourself to a mouse or trackpad when you have the convenient View button tools available on the left side of the screen.

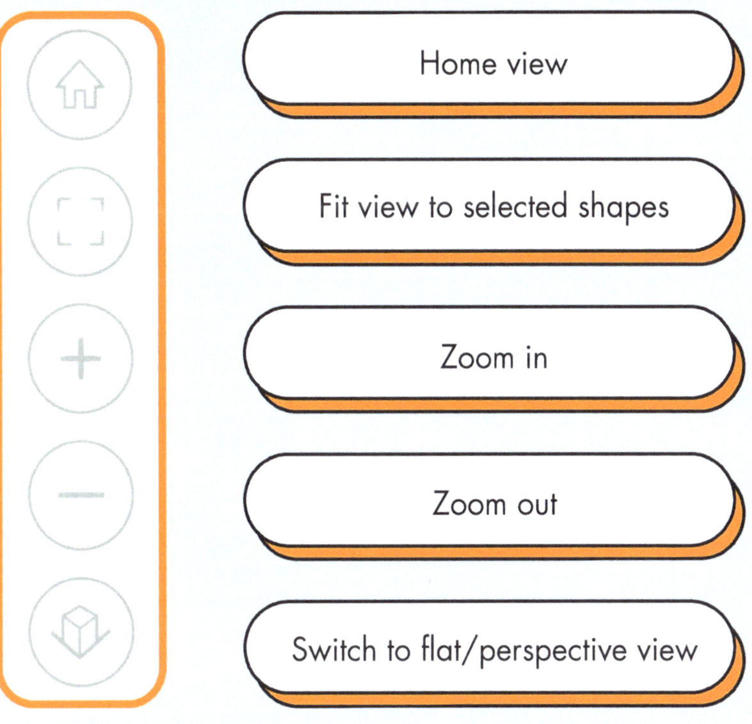

View It 

DO NOW

Go to the shape library and click the Basic Shape dropdown to show all the categories. Then click on Structures & Scenery and drag in the Apartment Building Ground Floor.

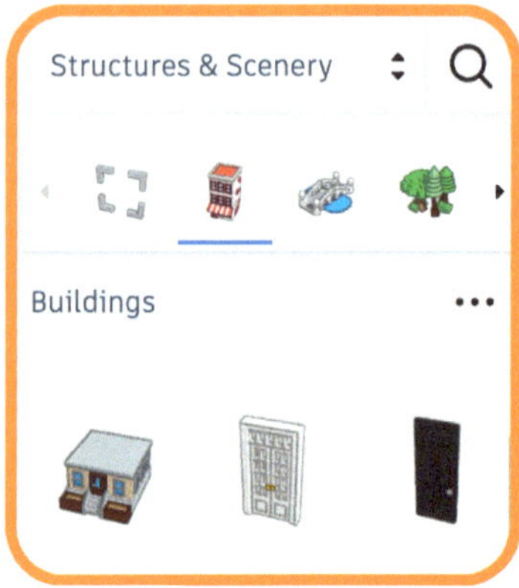

PLAY

Use your mouse and the View Buttons to:

1. **Zoom In**
2. **Fit All In View**
3. **Zoom Out**

PLAY

Click on the Top-Front-Right vertex then Fit All In View.

Toggle between the **Perspective / Flat** view.

What happens to the part of the design furthest away when in **Perspective View**?

....

Q: Count the total number of panes of glass the Apartment Building Ground Floor has.

 The lightbulb icon hides an object or design.

A: The numbers 5 & 6.
5 + 6 =

11

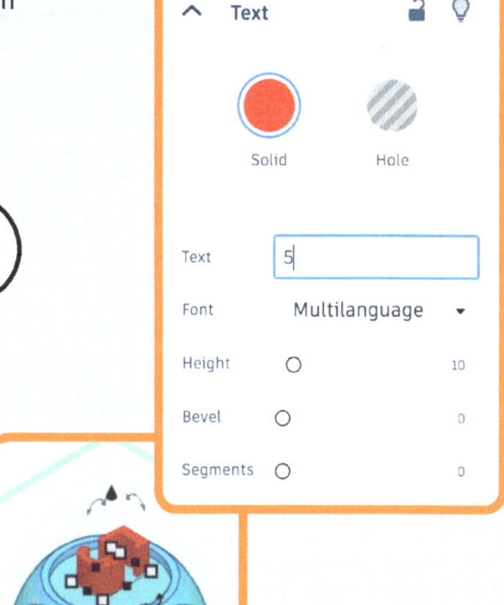

To add the missing numbers, students must find, select, and drag in the text tool.

They will need to place it using **Cruise** and then edit the Text to 5 or 6.

Finally, they must resize it using the white handles and adjust its position. And repeat.

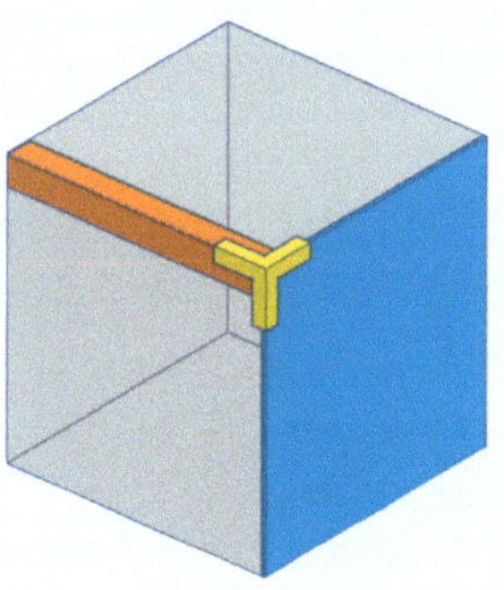

A: A cube has 12 edges, 6 faces, and 8 vertices.
12 + 6 + 8 =

26

https://t.ly/vwil2

A: When you remove perspective or change the view to orthographic (flat), the design stops appearing to get smaller as it gets further away. Using the flat view is helpful if you want to create an orthographic projection drawing, which an architect or mechanical engineer might create to share with a third party. A flat view is helpful here as it aids clarity of communication.

To create this drawing, turn off the Workplane and shadows via the settings menu.

Take screenshots or **Export** images of the front, top, and side views, then arrange them into the format and alignment you require.

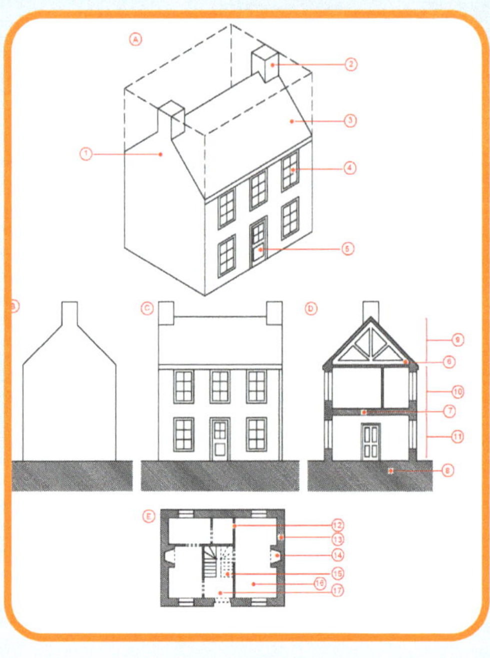

https://t.ly/parvZ

VIDEO

How to create an orthographic projection in Tinkercad

https://t.ly/parvZ

A: The total number of panes of glass the "apartment building ground floor" has

29

View It: iPad 

Tinkercad is great on an iPad too, but you'll need to master some different moves to get the most out of it.

PLAY

Tap on an object. Then tap it again. This selects it, then unselects it.

Press the screen with 1 finger and drag to **Orbit**.

PLAY

Tap on an object, then another, and then another. This adds them to the selection.

Press and move with 2 fingers to **Pan**.

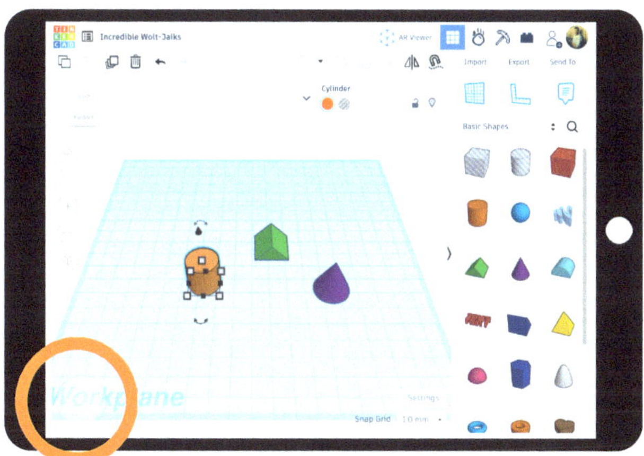

PLAY

Tap on an object. Tap and hold the button in the bottom left. This is an action modifier. For example, to change the scale from the center.

PLAY

Double tap, hold, and drag to create a selection box.

Pinch open or closed to **Zoom In** or **Zoom Out**.

View It: iPad 

Tinkercad on the iPad has one more special trick, Augmented Reality (AR)! Press the AR Viewer button and place your digital design into a physical space.

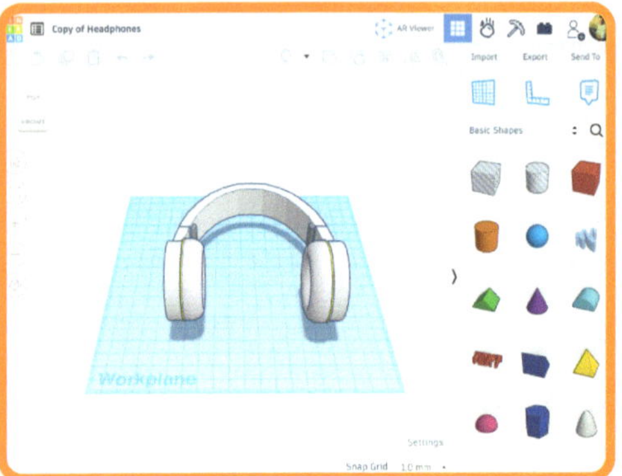

AR is a technology that maps digital information onto the real world.

It's used in applications like gaming, watching movies, and navigation.

PLAY

Search the **Gallery** for a pair of headphones.

Copy and Tinker It.

Use the **AR Viewer** to place it in your room.

Pinch the object to scale it.

Rotate It ↻

In Tinkercad, you can move shapes along 3 axes (X, Y, and Z).

Shapes can move left/right, up/down, and forward/backward.

They can also rotate around each axis. These make up the 6 DOFs (Degrees of Freedom).

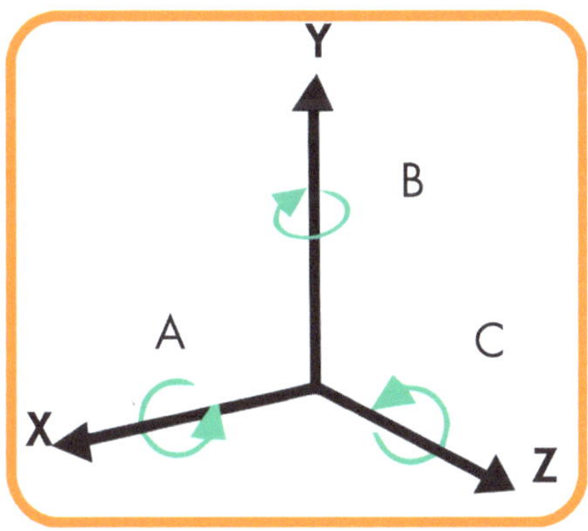

If you want to drive a screw into a piece of wood, it must move in 2 DOFs. It must travel into the wood while also rotating around the same axis.

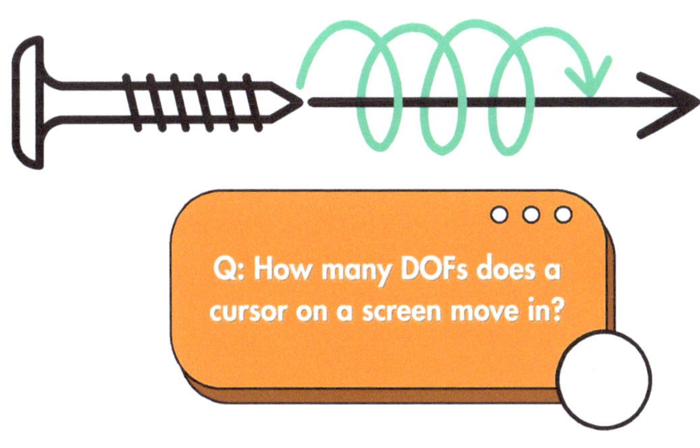

Rotate It ↻

When a shape is selected, notice the 3 curved arrows. Each represents a different axis to spin your shape around. Click and drag one, and your shape will rotate.

DO NOW

Save your previous design and start a new 3D Design.

Find the "Block head" model by searching for it 🔍 or via the **Creatures & Characters** dropdown.

Drag it onto the **Workplane**.

PLAY

You'll see 3 curved arrows when the shape is selected.

Click, hold, and move each arrow to rotate in each axis to nod, tilt, and shake his head!

Notice the **Protractor** that appears when rotating.

This gives you more control over how much it turns.

Rotate It ↻

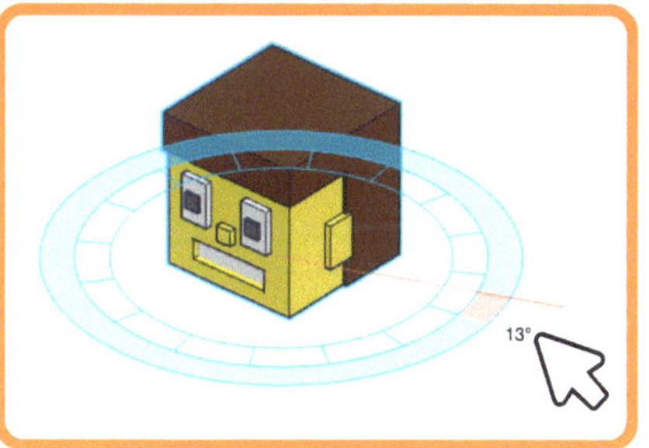

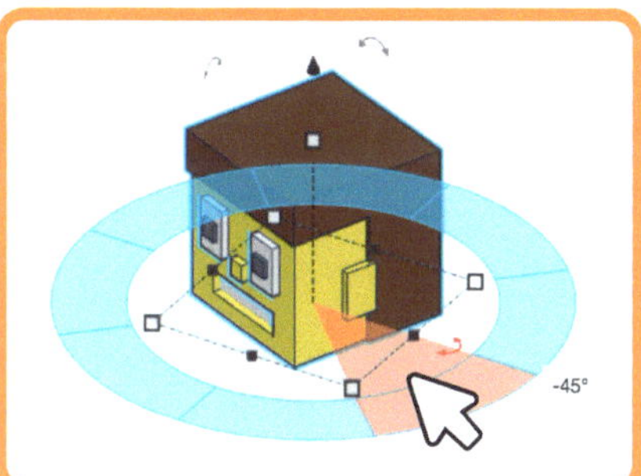

PLAY

Look closely! What happens differently when your mouse pointer is inside versus outside the **Protractor**?

....

....

Save it
Name it "Rotate It"

Rotate It 

Tinkercad also has its own museum of wonders called the Gallery. There are many designs that you can use and remix. Find the Gallery via the Dashboard in the top right-hand corner using the 🔍.

Search 3D Designs and more...

DO NOW

Search the gallery for "CADclass rotate"and press **Copy and Tinker** to make a copy.

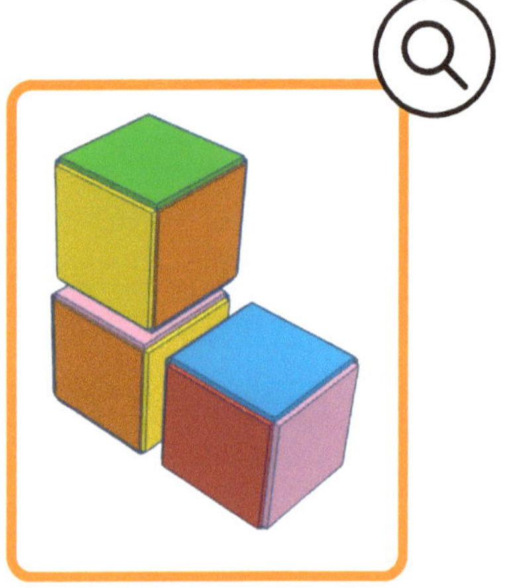

4

CHALLENGE

How long (in seconds) does it take you to rotate the cubes so all the sides have the same colors?

Save it
Name it "Speed Cube"

Solutions

The concept that you can move along an axis and rotate around that axis is at the core of advanced CNC (computer numeric control) concepts, such as 4 and 5-axis machining where a cutter moves in 3 axes, and the piece of material also rotates.

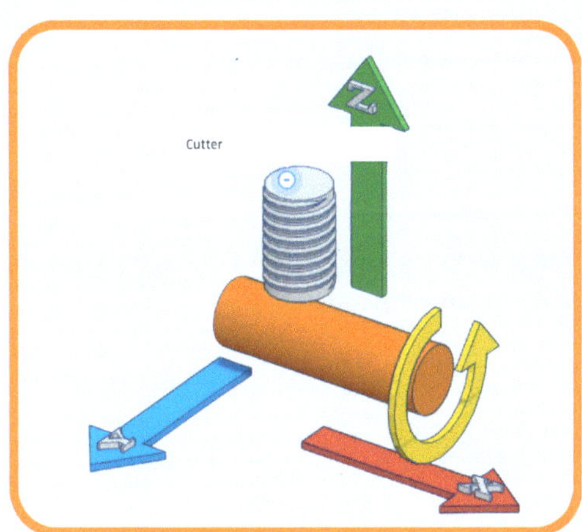

LINK

A Tinkercad model of a 4 axis machine
t.ly/wfK-r

4 axis CNC mill
t.ly/ewEdJ

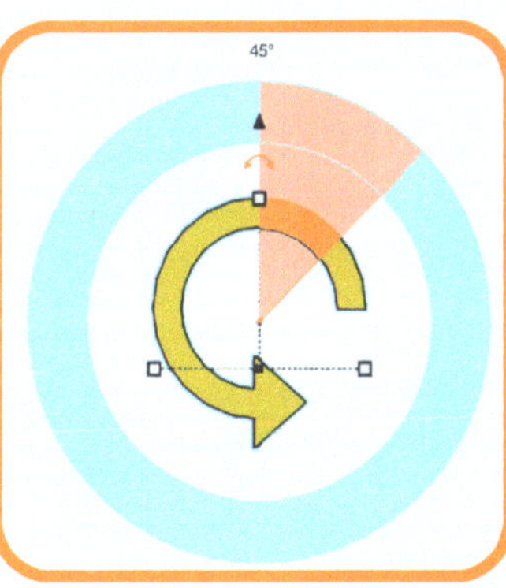

A cursor on a screen moves with 2 degrees of freedom in the X and Y axes

If the cursor is inside the Protractor, it will rotate in 22.5° increments. Outside the outer circle, it will move 1° at a time. You can still type in the exact value you require. Minus (-) is an anti-clockwise rotation. Holding Shift makes it snap to 45° increments.

Size It 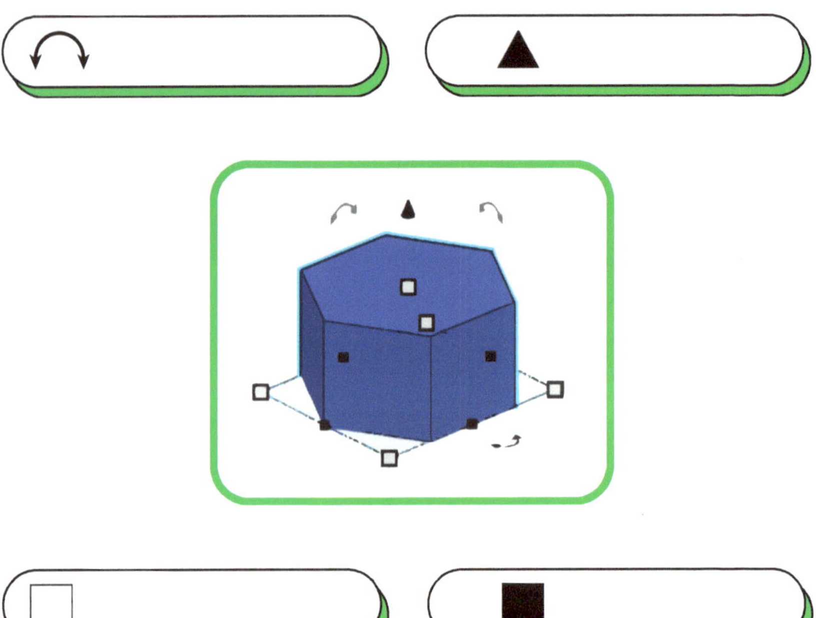

It's essential to resize/scale shapes to explore form and proportion or to make your designs fit with other objects.

DO NOW

Create a new 3D Design and drag in a Polygon. Select it.

Click on and test each of these symbols. Describe what they do in the box.

DO NOW

Try holding **Shift** while trying some of these actions to see if there is anything different.

Size It 

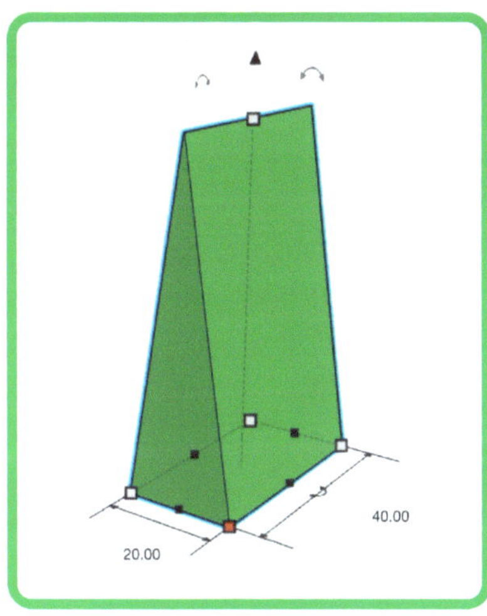

DO NOW

You can also resize shapes to a specific dimension by typing a number into the dimension box.

Drag a Roof onto the **Workplane** and make it:

- 20.0 mm wide
- 40.0 mm deep
- 60.0 mm tall

PLAY

Start a new 3D Design. Drag in a blue Sphere and make a few copies.

Click on the white or black handles and a dimension box pops up. Type in any number.

Play with all the resizing options to make a pile of magic stones!

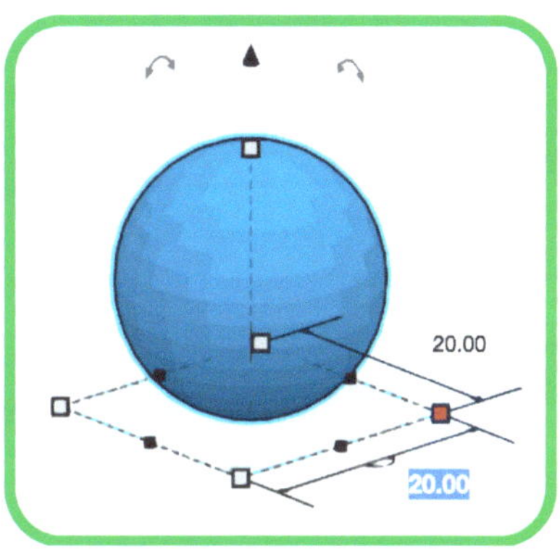

Save it
Name it "Size It"

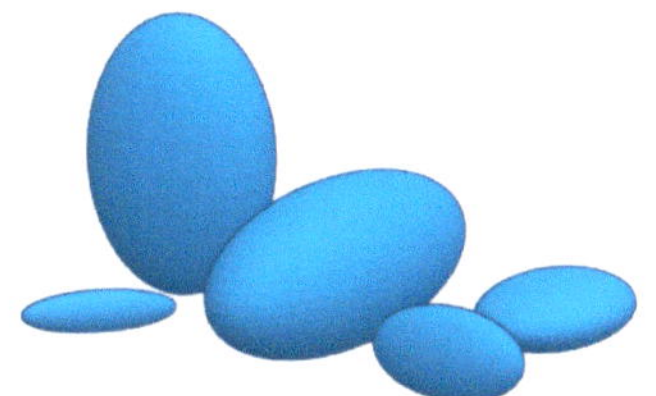

Size It 

White handles let you resize in 2 directions simultaneously, while the black handles only let you resize one side at a time.

Action modifier buttons add superpowers: Shift and Alt (or option). On an iPad, this is the white button in the screen's bottom left corner.

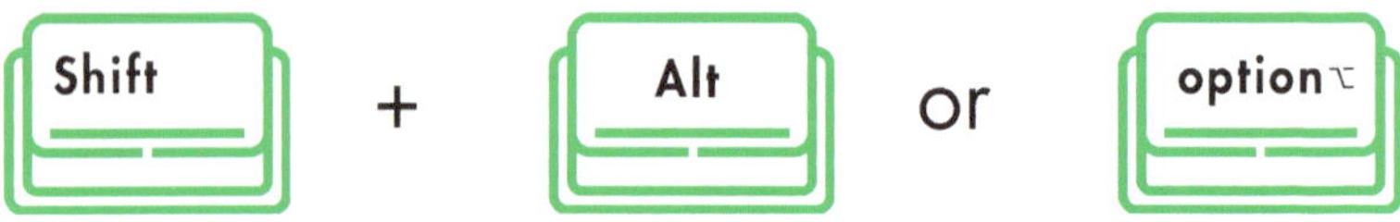

DO NOW

Create a new 3D Design. Change the view so you can look down on the Workplane from above. Click and drag the orange Tube into place so it frames the letter W.

PLAY

Select the Tube, hold **Shift**, and drag the white square. Notice the direction the Tube scales in.

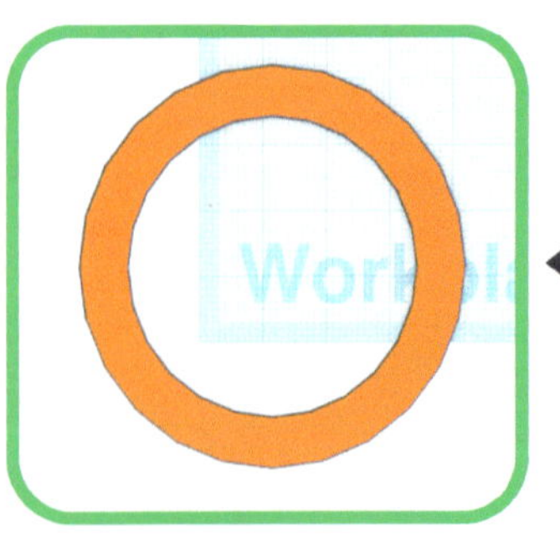

PLAY

Press Undo. Repeat the action but hold Shift + Alt / option and drag a white square. You can still see the letter W because it scaled from the center, not one side.

Size It

DO NOW

Open a new 3D Design.

Go to the library and use the top dropdown menu to find **Creatures & Characters**.

Use the arrows on the first sub-menu to scroll across. Select **Animals**.

Use your searching, moving, and resizing skills to attempt Challenge 5.

5

CHALLENGE

Create an alliterated zoo of strangely scaled animals: a flat frog, a big bee, a long llama, a stretched seal...

Save it
Name it "Animal Zoo" 

Solutions 

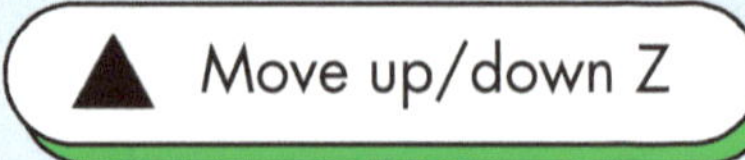

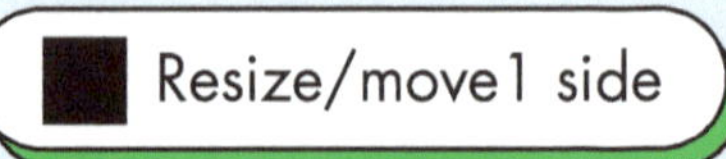

Holding the Shift or Alt/option is known as an **Action Modifier** - in this case, it preserves the original proportions (or makes it bigger or smaller at the same rate). If you have a keyboard, "Shift" is the action modifier. If you are using the iPad app, the Action Modifier button is in the bottom left corner and works like the Shift key.

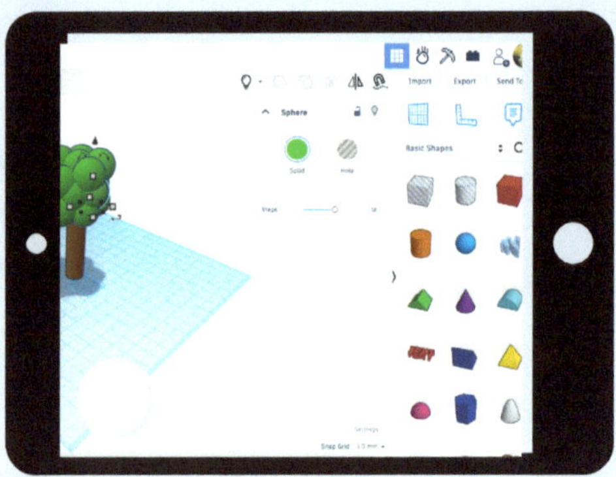

Ways you can use size/resize:

- Design a full-size chair, then resize it by a scale of 1:6. This is known as the "play scale," a proportion suitable for toys. Follow this link for information on scale. t.ly/K6On3
- Try to make mash-up designs using parts from the library that have been designed at different scales, e.g., a whale wearing a hat.

VIDEO

A House for Absolute Beginners iPad Tutorial
t.ly/9seYf

Fill in the Shortcut Gaps

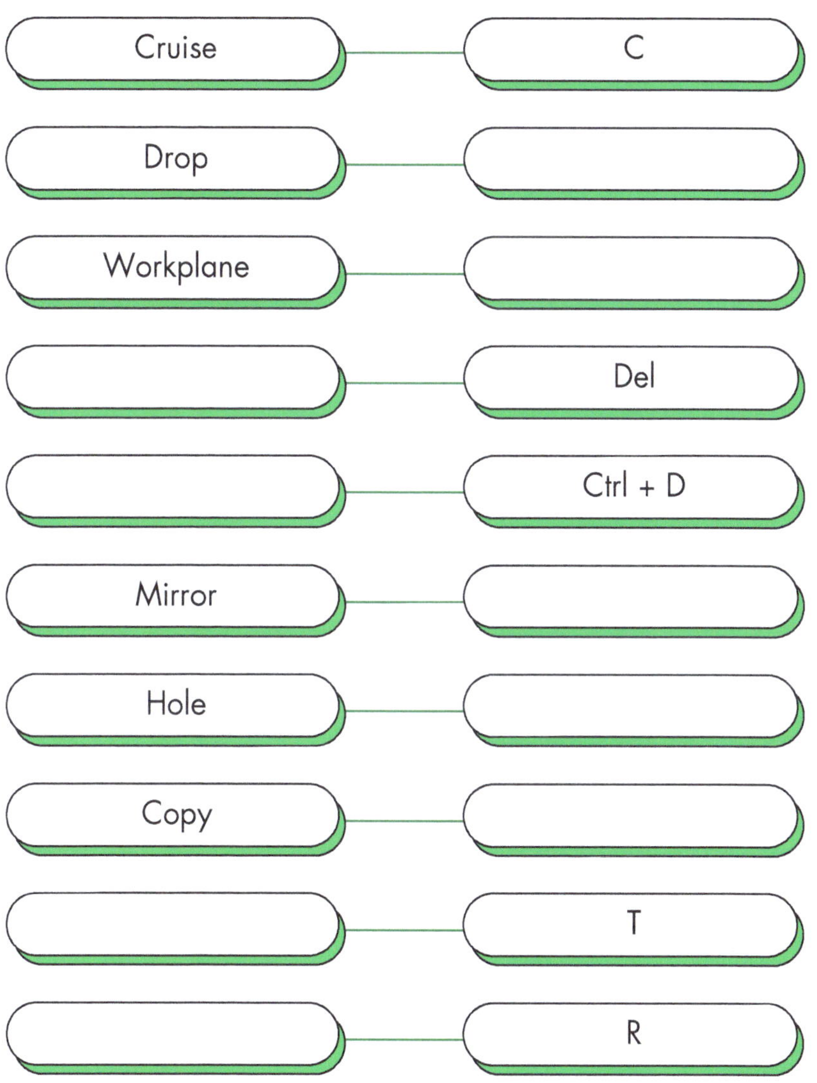

Solutions 

Cruise	C
Drop	D
Workplane	W
Delete	Del
Duplicate and Repeat	Ctrl + D
Mirror	M
Hole	H
Copy	Ctrl + C
Make Transparent	T
Place Ruler	R

Group It

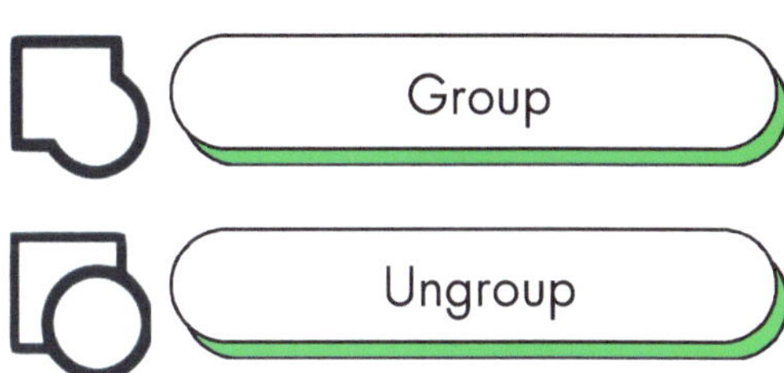

The Group tool combines shapes into new objects. If one of those shapes is a Hole, it removes material from the other shape(s). These are the 2 buttons you need:

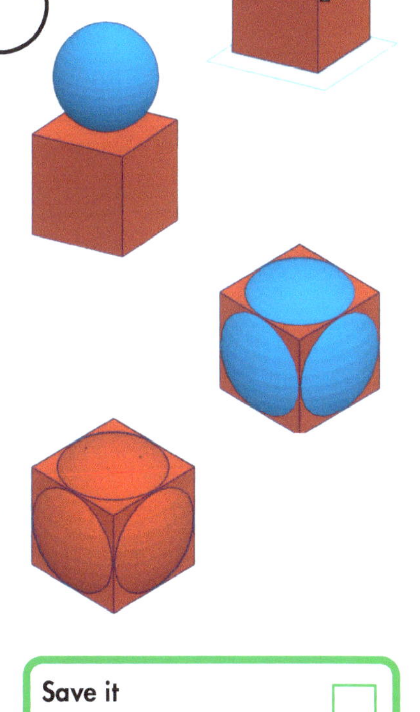

PLAY

Create a new 3D Design.

Drag a red cube onto the **Workplane** and place a blue Sphere on top of it.

Resize the Sphere to be 28 mm in all directions.

Move the Sphere so it's inside the cube.

Select both shapes (hold Shift while clicking) and press **Group**.

Now you have a new object!

Save it
Name it "Convex Cube"

Group It 

1. Create a new 3D Design. Search for "Signet Ring Blank" and drag it onto the Workplane.

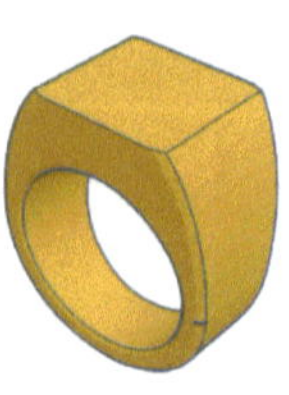

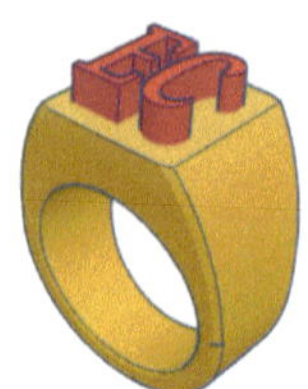

2. Drag text onto the ring, change it to your initials, and resize it.

3. Select and move the Text down through the ring surface with   .

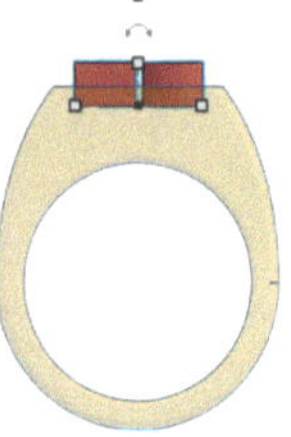

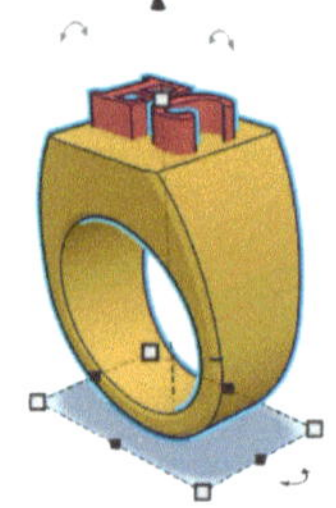

4. Select both shapes by holding Shift when clicking and **Group** them. Note the blue outline on both selected objects.

5. Now you have a ring with "embossed" letters.

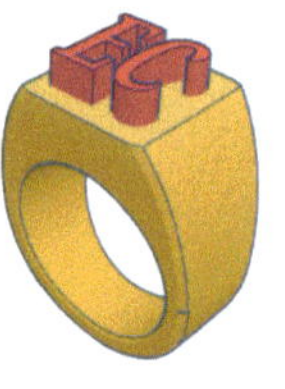

6. When you grouped the shapes they might have changed color to match the first part selected. To keep the original colors click **Solid** > then **Multicolor**.

> **Save it**
> Name it "[name] Ring"

Solutions 

Tinkercad uses some "Boolean operations" (AND, OR, NOT, XOR etc), also known as Constructive Solid Geometry (CSG). The **Group** tool enables the following Boolean operations: **Union:** combine 2 objects into a new one. **Subtraction**: Subtract one object from another to create a new object. Read more here: t.ly/G7B9z

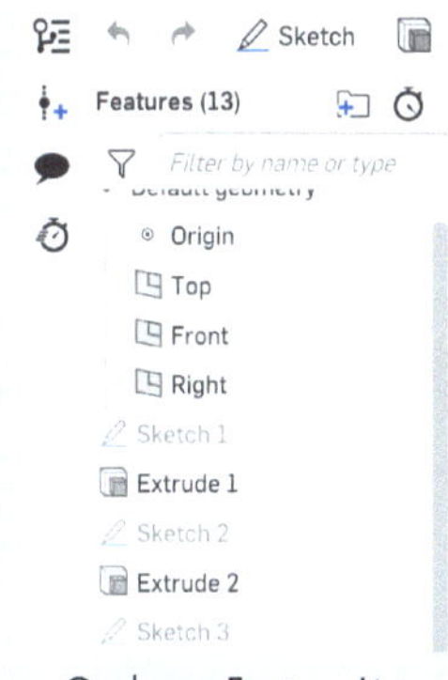

Onshape Feature List

Using **Ungroup** is an effective way to reverse engineer other designs from the Gallery. Many advanced CAD programs use a graphical interface that shows the progress in chronological stages of how a design was constructed. In Onshape this is called the Feature List and in Fusion it's called the Timeline.

Fusion's Timeline

Grouped telephone by user ZDP189

https://t.ly/H–Er

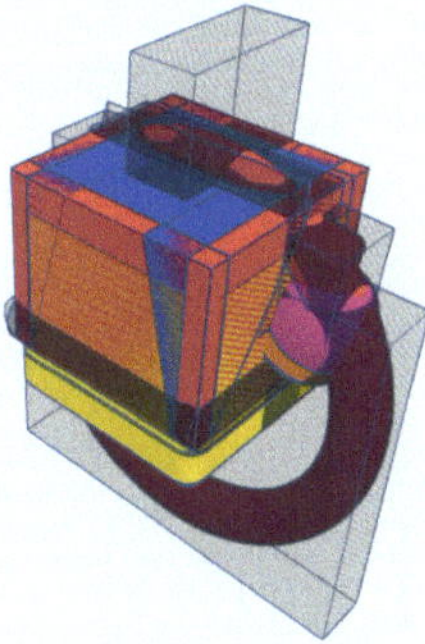

Ungrouped

It's easier to resize a grouped multi-part design.

When you group shapes they might change color to match the first part selected.

To keep the original colors click **Solid** > then **Multicolor**

Multicolor

Copy It

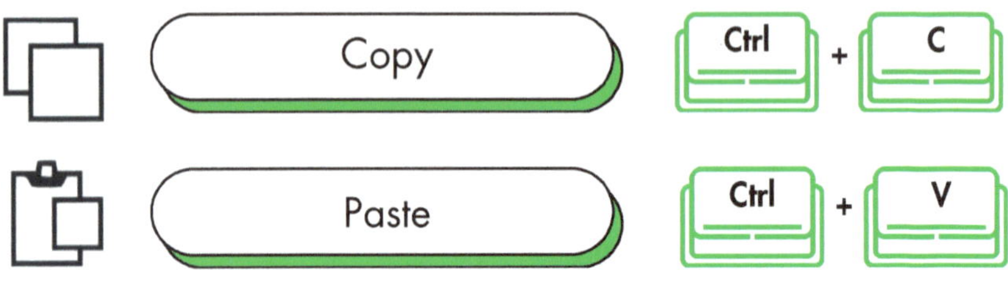

Like in other software, you can make copies of all or part of your designs using standard Copy and Paste keyboard shortcuts.

	Copy	Ctrl + C
	Paste	Ctrl + V

DO NOW

Go to the Gallery, search 🔍 for "CADclass alphabet", and press **Copy and Tinker**.

Copy and Tinker

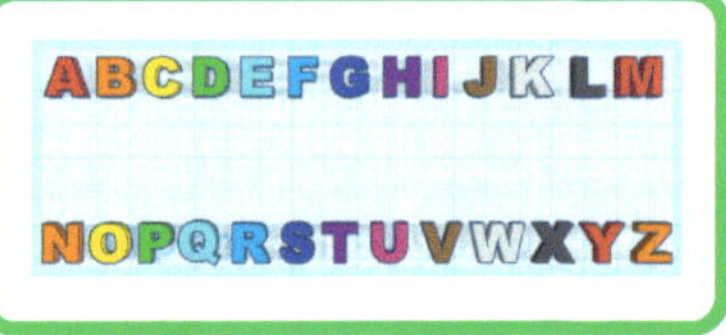

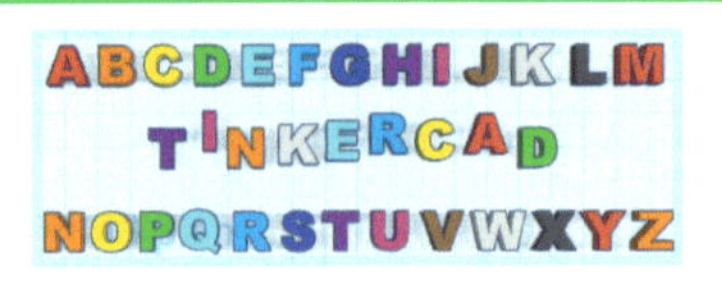

Do your letters look a bit wonky?

Don't worry, we'll be exploring how to line them up using the **Align** tool soon.

PLAY

Practice **Copy** and **Pasting** letters – keep the alphabet and create the word TINKERCAD.

Try to use both the onscreen buttons and and the keyboard shortcuts.

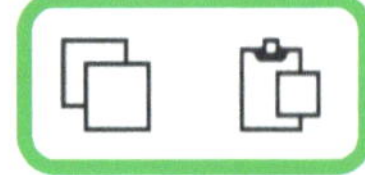

Copy It

DO NOW

Open a new 3D Design. Find one of these figures from the Creatures & Characters dropdown menu in the Library and drag it onto the Workplane.

PLAY

Practice using the keyboard arrow keys to move the figure left and right.

Edit the distance the character moves with each click by changing the **Snap Grid** to 5.0 mm.

Off	
0.1 mm	
0.25 mm	
0.5 mm	
1.0 mm	
2.0 mm	
5.0 mm	
Brick	
Snap Grid	1.0 mm ▲

CHALLENGE

6

Use a character to make a triangle using only Copy + Paste + Move.

What is the fewest clicks you can do it in?

Solutions 

The **Copy**, **Cut,** and **Paste** commands play a crucial role in human-computer interaction (HCI) and the design of user interfaces. These commands facilitate interprocess communication by enabling data transfer within a computer's user interface. **Copy** generates a duplicate whereby the selected data is temporarily stored in an area known as the clipboard. The clipboard data can be inserted wherever a **Paste** command is executed and often to other programs.

The names are metaphors based on the physical procedures used in print editing when people cut from a page with scissors and pasted it onto another page.

These keyboard shortcuts also feature in many software packages:

- Control-X (or   +X) to **Cut**
- Control-C (or   +C) to **Copy**
- Control-V (or   +V) to **Paste**
- Control-Z (or   +Z) to **Undo**

VIDEO

The Lost Art of Paste-Up
London Review of Books

t.ly/cOkd7

6

CHALLENGE

By grouping and copying multiple parts - and increasing the grid size you can minimise clicks. 30 is a great score.

≈30

We will look at copying from other Tinkercad designs later in the book.

Duplicate It 

The Duplicate tool is similar to the Copy tool, but with a twist. It remembers your last move and mimics it. So, not only does it copy and paste selected objects, but it also repeats your previous action.

DO NOW

1. Start a new 3D Design.
2. Find and insert a Star.
3. Select the shape.
4. Click **Duplicate**.
5. **Rotate** it and move it.
6. Click **Duplicate** repeatedly.

PLAY

Create a spiral staircase from a single resized box.

💡 Don't forget to move in all 3 axes and rotate too!

Q: Ctrl + ? is the shortcut key for Duplicate?

Save it
Name it "Duplicate It"

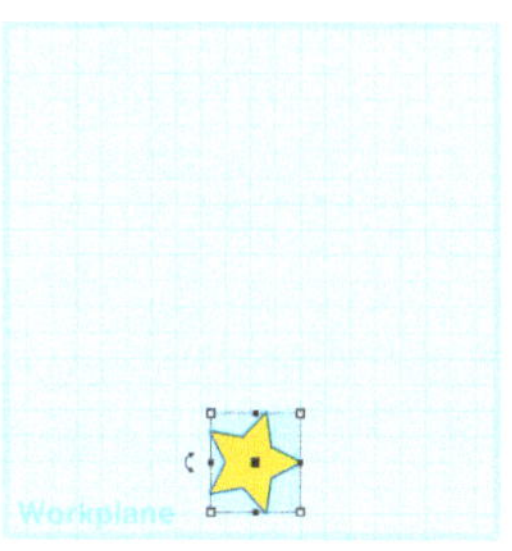

Insert and select Star

Press **Duplicate** and move the Star

Press **Duplicate** again and again…

Hide It 

Sometimes you'll want to hide shapes rather than delete them forever. Maybe there's too much design magic happening on the screen. Don't get rid of it, hide it!

DO NOW

Search the gallery for "CADclass 16 segment display" and press **Copy and Tinker** to make a copy.

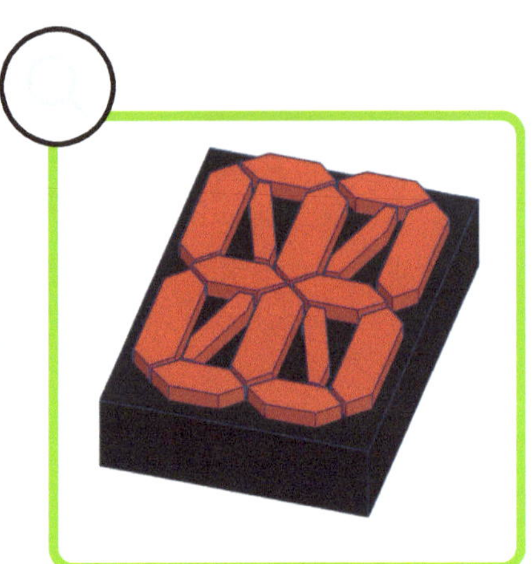

Copy and Tinker

PLAY

Practice selecting segments by:

1. Holding **Shift** and clicking shapes to select multiple segments.

2. Using the **Hide** tool, try to create your name.

Note: If you accidentally select the wrong segment, keep holding Shift and press it again to deselect it.

Save it
Name it "16 Segment"

Hide It

Other times, you'll want something in between Solid and Hidden. Go into the color menu and find the **Transparent** checkbox, or use the keyboard shortcut **T** to make it look like water or glass.

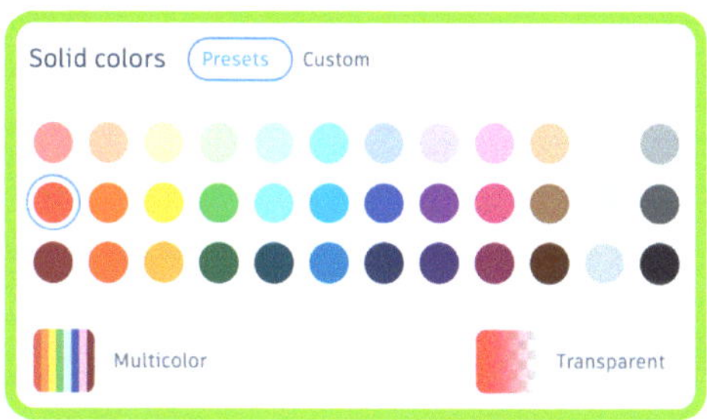

The Shell Game is a trick often seen in performances and at fairs involving a ball and 3 cups. In this game, a player must guess which cup the ball is under. The operator manipulates the game to deceive the player, often using sleight of hand.

7

CHALLENGE

Make a game by grouping a ball inside one of 3 shapes. Show it using transparency. Jumble them & unhide to reveal it.

Note: Use the **Group** tool to join the ball and its Pyramid so they move together.

Align It 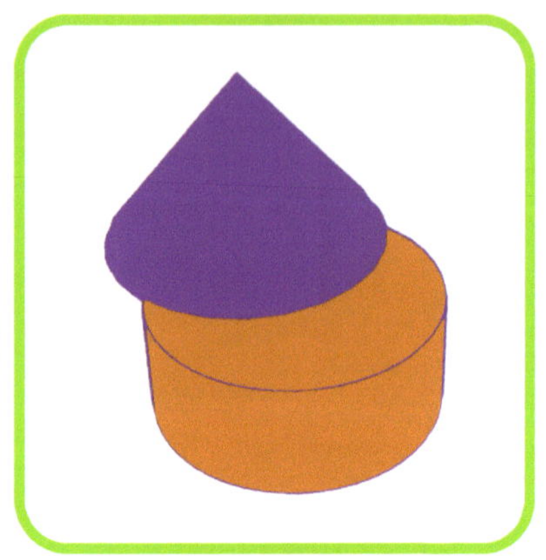

Using the Align tool or the keyboard shortcut L, you can bring 2 or more shapes into perfect alignment. It works in all 3 dimensions (X, Y, Z).

DO NOW

1. Start a new 3D Design.

2. Grab a Cylinder and make it 50.0 x 50.0 mm wide and 20.0 mm in height.

3. Grab a Cone and drag it roughly onto the top face of the Cylinder. Make it 50.0 x 50.0 mm wide and 30.0 mm tall.

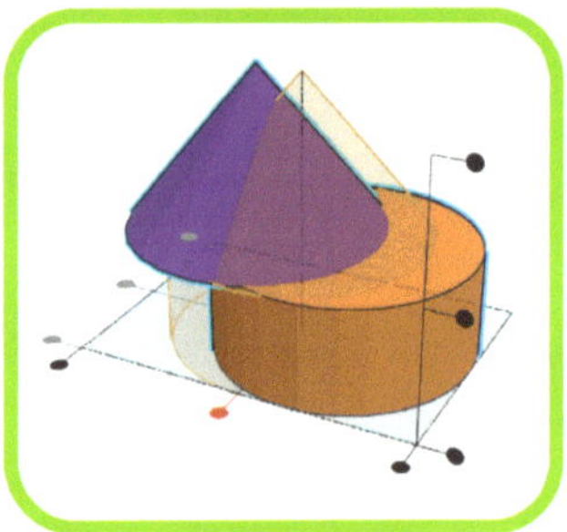

4. Select both objects and press the **Align** button.

5. Click the middle ● on the Workplane and notice how the Cone aligns to the center of the Cylinder.

6. Press **Undo** and select both shapes again.

7. Press the top ● on the Z (   ) axis first and it'll align to the top of the Cone. The order of operation is very important!

Align It

8. Click **Undo**, re-select both shapes, and click **Align**.

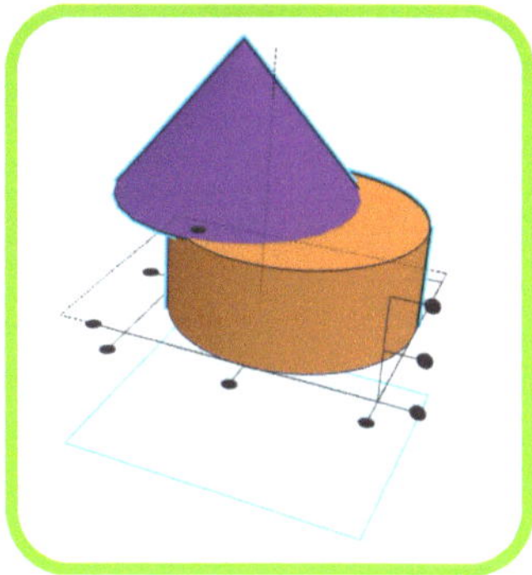

9. Click the Cylinder *again* - this makes it a reference, and you'll notice the alignment nodes ● are only surrounding it, so it will not move.

10. Press any ● and see what happens!

PLAY

Search the gallery for "CADclass chess!" and press **Copy and Tinker** to open the design.

Copy and Tinker

8

CHALLENGE

Hold the Shift key while selecting a moved piece and an unmoved pawn of the same color, then use Align to reset the game.

Refresher:

Sketch the **Duplicate** icon here

Refresher:

Sketch the **Ungroup** icon here

Q: Ctrl + ? is the shortcut key for Hide?

Refresher:

Sketch the **Un/Hide** icon here

Refresher:

Sketch the **Copy** icon here

Solutions 

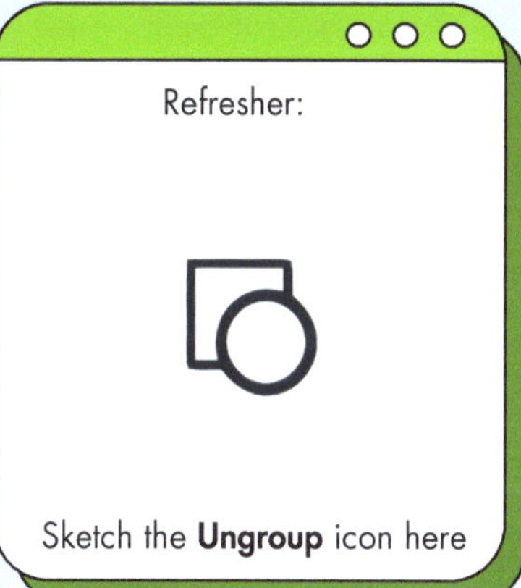

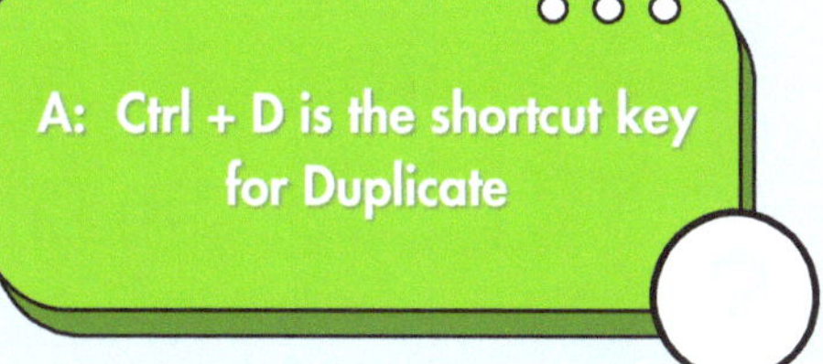

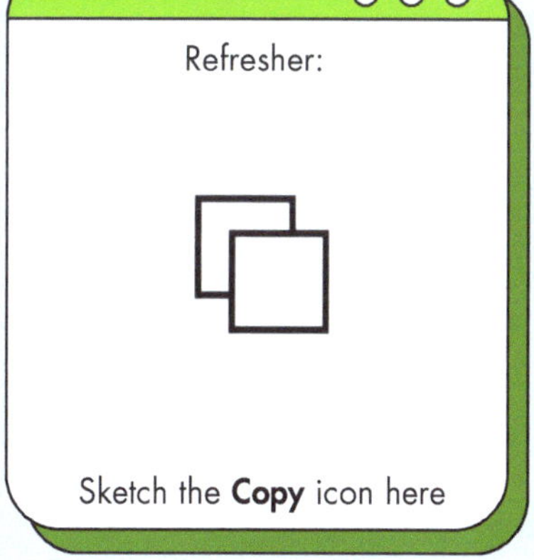

Create Holes

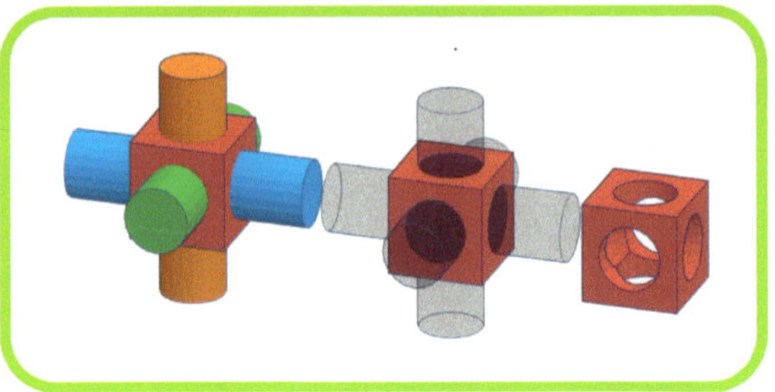

Until now, you've been creating by adding parts, like building with blocks. But you can also create by subtracting using Holes. This tool removes material from a solid when grouped. Holes are striped, grey, and semi-transparent.

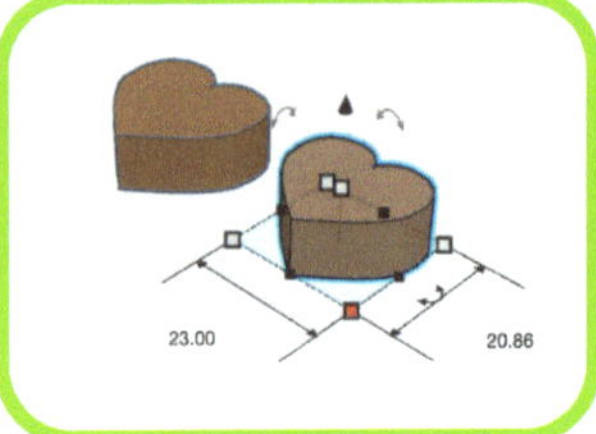

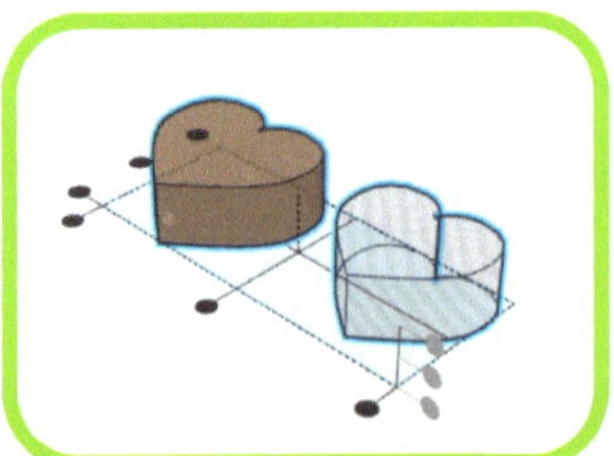

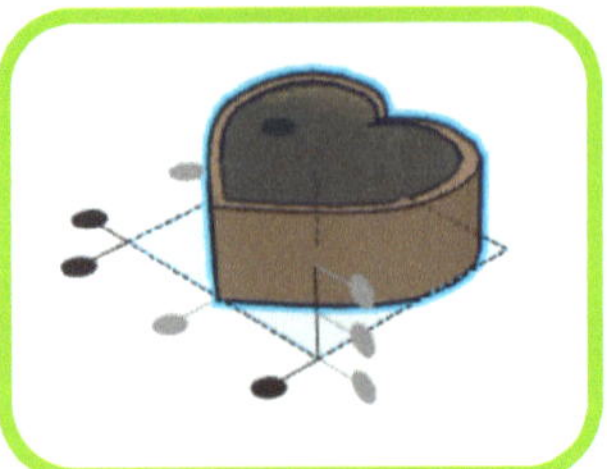

DO NOW

1. Start a new 3D Design.
2. Drag in a Heart shape from the Gallery and Copy & Paste it so there are 2.
3. Resize one so it's 3.0 mm less in both the X and Y axes.
4. Make it a **Hole**.
5. **Align** and **Group** them to make a heart-shaped cookie cutter! 🍪

Q: Can ANY shape become a hole? Y or N

Solutions 

Tinkercad is based on the constructive solid geometry (CSG) method of modeling, which allows the designer to construct solid objects out of "primitive" 3D shapes like Boxes and cylinders. This process is beginner-friendly and is a building block for advanced CAD concepts.

Constructive solid geometry allows a designer to create complex objects using Boolean Operators to combine simpler objects, potentially generating complex objects by combining a number of "primitive" ones. This is like permanently combining simple building blocks to make vastly complex 3D forms.

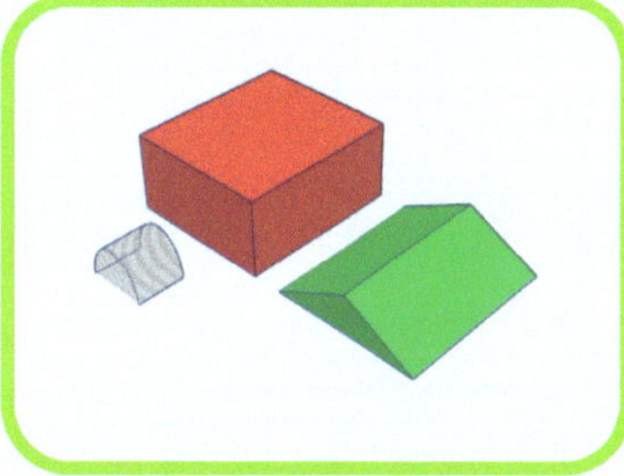

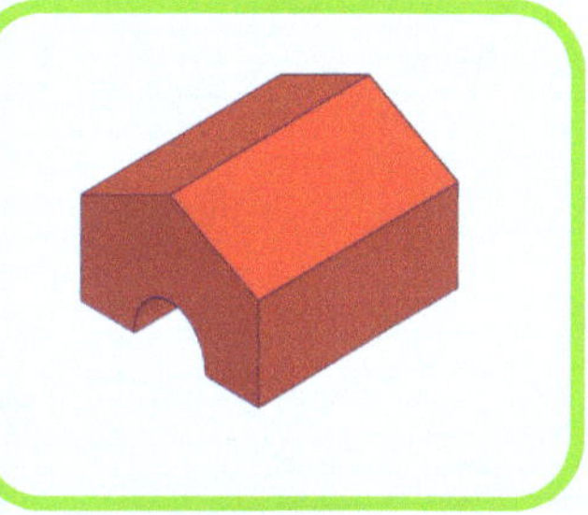

Advantages of CSG:

It's fast and intuitive.
The data behind it is small,
meaning it can work in an
internet browser.
Designs can be ungrouped.

Limitations of CSG:

Limited in creating curves.
Complex shapes may require
many steps.

Rename

Q: Hey Tinkercad, what's with the weird names?

A: Tinkercad automatically generates a unique 3-word name so files don't get mixed up. You can change it using one of these methods.

DO NOW

Double click on the name and delete it. Update it with something that identifies your name, what it is, and the version:

Ed_cookiecutter_heart_V1

PLAY

You can also rename your design via the Dashboard.

Get there by pressing the Tinkercad logo in the top left corner.

Then press the gear icon in the top right of the preview tile, select Properties, and change the name.

Use one of your existing designs to practice this.

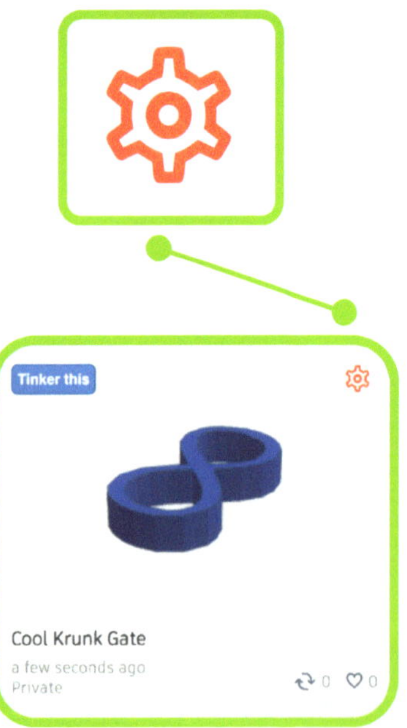

Search Shapes 🔍

Searching for pre-made shapes is at the heart of Tinkercad. This tool allows you to find and use hundreds of models that would otherwise take hours or days to create.

Q: How many types of batteries are there?

2   6   9   25

What is the BIGGEST and the *smallest* design you can find in the library (if it was real)?

Q: What is the theme of the OMSI collection? (A) Furniture (B) Space (C) Construction.

....

....

9

CHALLENGE

Create a tiny desert island using only shapes from the Library?

Mirror ◁|▷

You've gone left and right, up and down. Now let's go back-to-front, over-and-over! Mirror allows you to flip your design using the black arrows that appear when you click the Mirror icon. ◁|▷

Circle all the symmetrical letters :

A B C D E F G H I
J K L M N O P Q R
S T U V W X Y Z

List some symmetrical numbers 1-100:

Q: What is is the shortcut key for Mirror?

Mirror

Use the **Text** tool and write MOM.

Change the font to sans to remove the serifs (the little tails on the letters shown in the image to the left).

Mirror the word and find the hidden word. What is it?

....

10

CHALLENGE

Find an asymmetrical object from the Gallery and "animate it" by quickly Mirroring it.

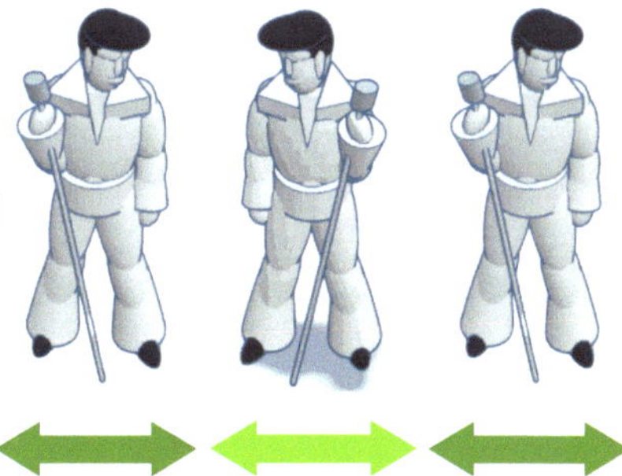

Save it
Name it "Mirror"

A: How many types of batteries are there?
2   6   9   25

6

Look closely, as some are battery boxes!

The Oregon Museum of Science and Industry inspires curiosity through engaging science learning experiences: omsi.edu/

A: What is the theme of the OMSI collection? (A) Furniture (B) Space (C) Construction

A

A: M is the shortcut key for Mirror.

M

Remember, hovering your mouse over any of the buttons should reveal its name and shortcut (if it has one).

Horizontally symmetrical:
B C D E H I K O X

Vertically symmetrical:
A H I M O T U V W X Y

Symmetrical numbers:
0, 3, 8, 69, 88, 96

MOM
WOW

MOM/WOW is a type Ambigram. Read about others here:
en.wikipedia.org/wiki/Ambigram

Match the Icon & Word

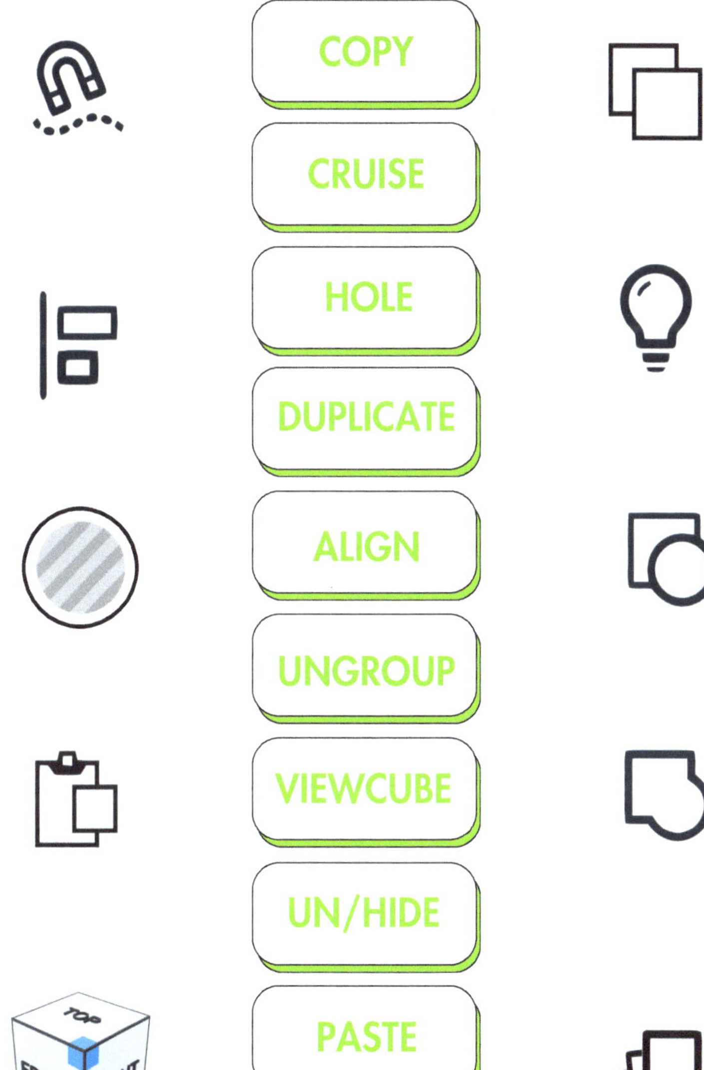

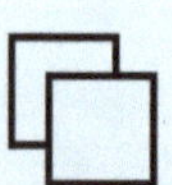
COPY

CRUISE

HOLE

DUPLICATE

ALIGN

UNGROUP

VIEWCUBE

UN/HIDE

PASTE

GROUP

Use the Grid 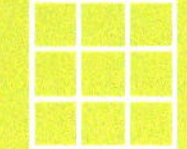

Grids help you visualize the distance between shapes, like squares on graph paper. Snap Grid changes the spacing of those squares on your Workplane. When the Snap Grid is on, shapes align to the lines. You can change the spacing and turn the Grid on/off via the button in the bottom right corner.

1. Change the **Snap Grid** to 5.0 mm spacing.

2. Create 1 white cube 25.0 x 25.0 x 25.0 mm.

3. Create 1 black cube 25.0 x 25.0 x 25.0 mm.

4. **Align** the black and the white cube

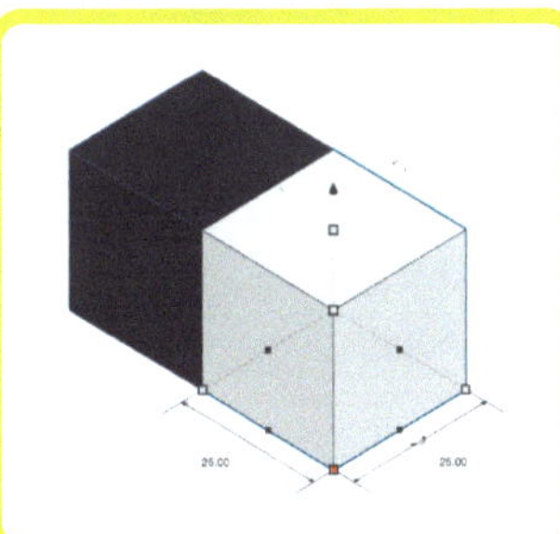

11

CHALLENGE

Make a chess board using the keyboard keys by Copy & Pasting 2 cubes at the same time. Hint: Copy + Paste + + M.

Number the Features

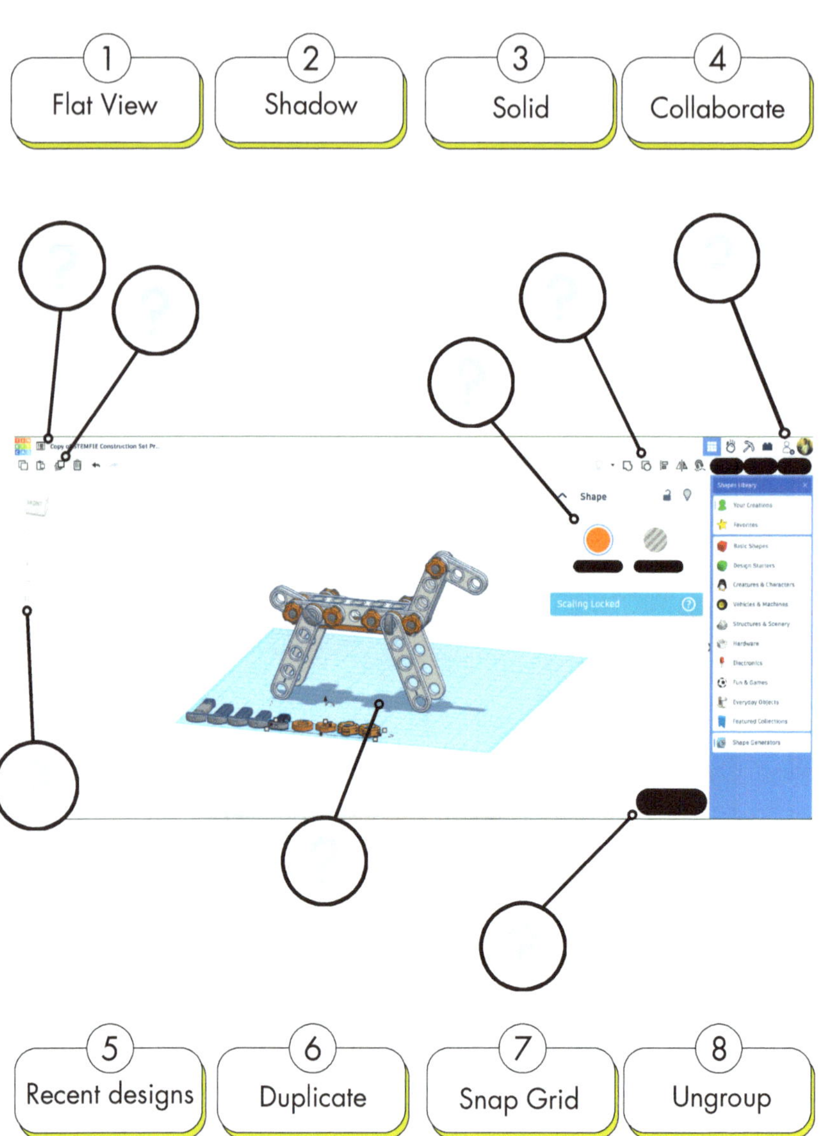

1 Flat View

2 Shadow

3 Solid

4 Collaborate

5 Recent designs

6 Duplicate

7 Snap Grid

8 Ungroup

Solutions

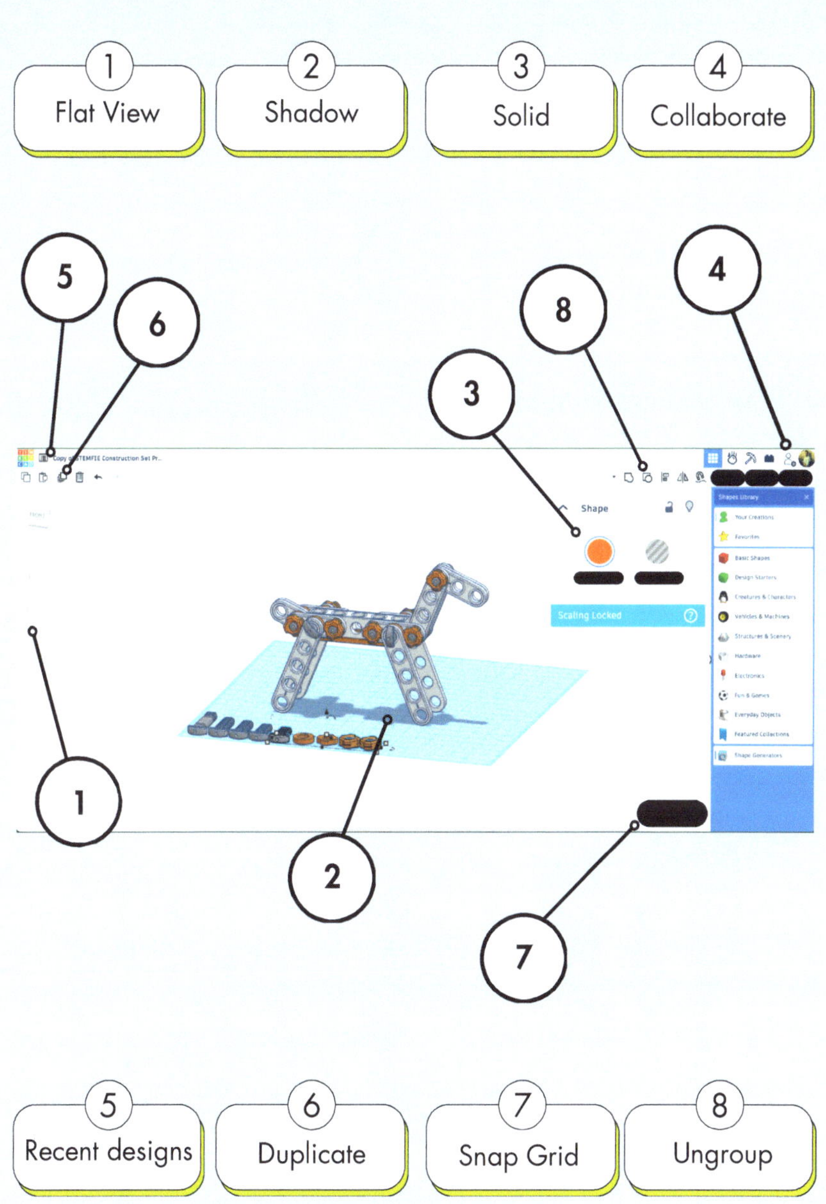

Workplanes

A Workplane is like a piece of paper you place on the surface of a shape to connect another shape to its surface. Cruise mode automatically does this when you drag in a new shape, but you can add more yourself!

DO NOW

1. Drag the Icosahedron onto the Workplane.

2. Scale it to approximately a quarter of the Workplane, keeping its proportions.

HINT: use the Action Modifier keyboard key.

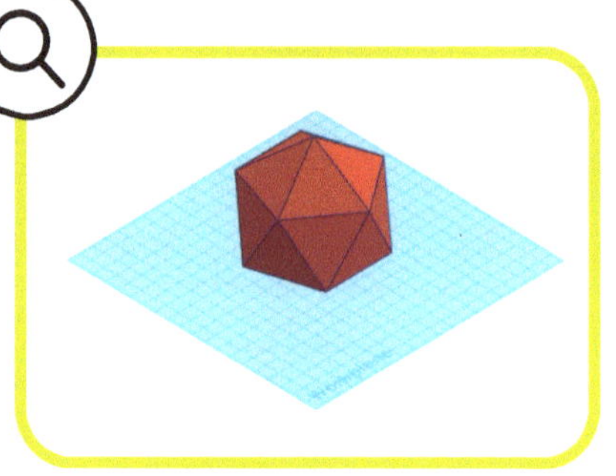

PLAY

3. Drag and scale other shapes onto the Icosahedron to create a fun character.

Check out the free trial video by HL Mod Tech on the CADclass website!

http://cadclass.org/courses/tinkercad

Workplanes 

Sometimes aligning objects is tricky so let's look at how you can use Workplanes to help.

1. Drag a Box on to the Workplane and make it orange.

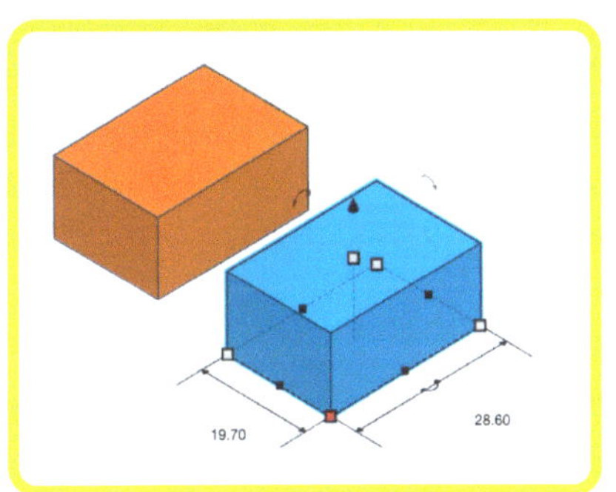

2. Resize it to: 19.7 x 28.6 x 13.1 mm.

3. Copy and Paste it to make a duplicate and make it blue.

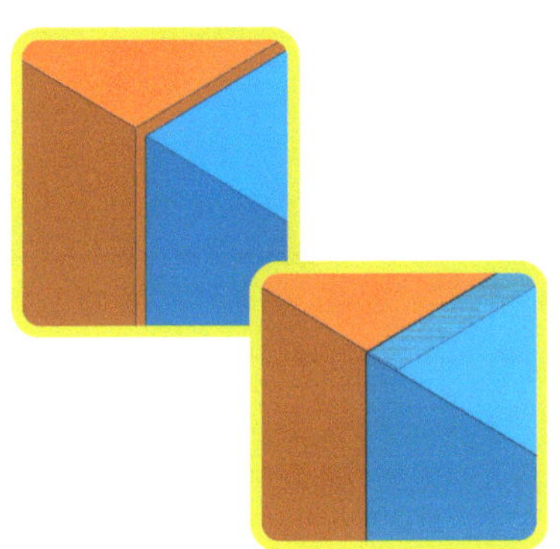

4. Align the Boxes using the **Align** tool.

5. Now Align them using the mouse keys and the Snap Grid.

When you Zoom in you'll see you always have a gap or an overlap because of the tricky dimensions.

6. Press **W** for Workplane and place new Workplane on the side of the orange Box.

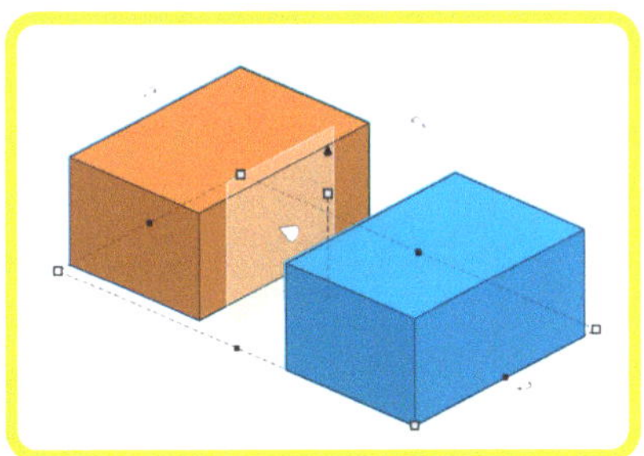

Workplanes 

DO NOW

7. Select the other Box and press **D** to drop the blue Box onto the new Workplane.

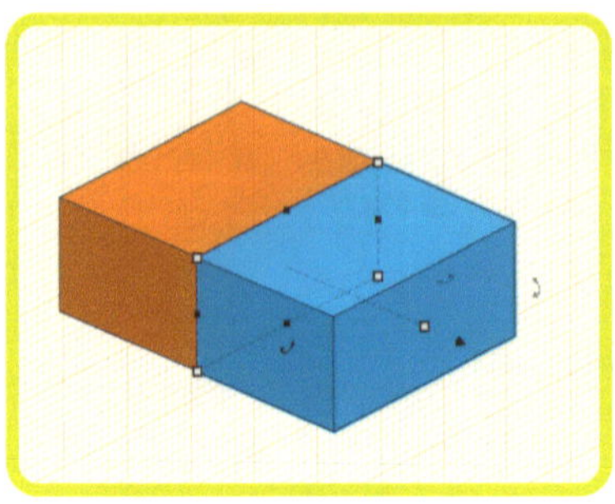

8. Press **W** again and place the Workplane back on the original Workplane. The new one will disappear

9. Zoom In to check for a gap or overlap.

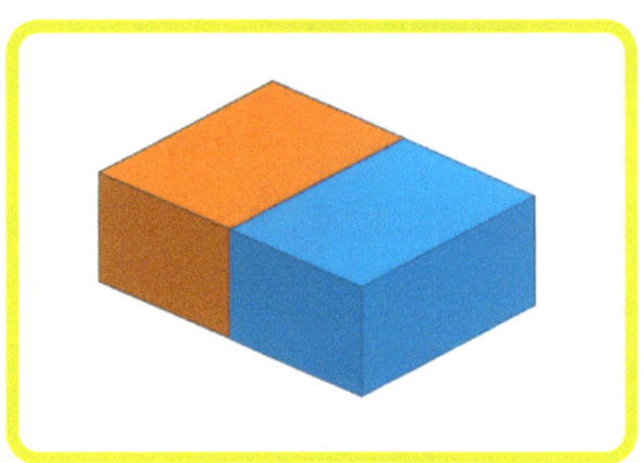

Save it
Name it "Aligned"

Measure It 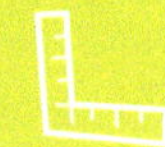

You know how to size objects with the black and white handles and the dimension box. But what if you need to know specific measurements? The Ruler is the tool you'll need.

DO NOW

- Find the Micro:bit in the **Shape Library** and drag it onto the Workplane.
- Click the **Ruler** and place it away from the bottom left corner.
- Select the Micro:bit to measure it.

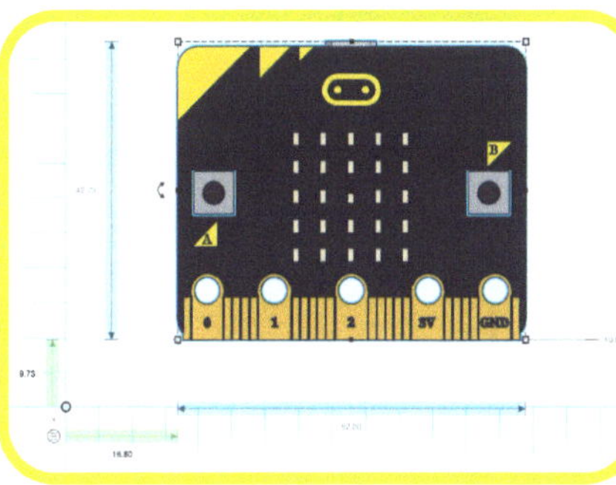

The blue dimensions are **absolute** to the part.

The green dimensions are **relative** to the origin of the Ruler.

PLAY

1. Place the Ruler near the bottom corner of the Micro:bit.
2. Select the Micro:bit and change the green dimensions (relative) to 0.0 mm to snap its corner to the origin.
3. Check the Micro:bit width and height. Check your answers here: en.wikipedia.org/wiki/Micro_Bit

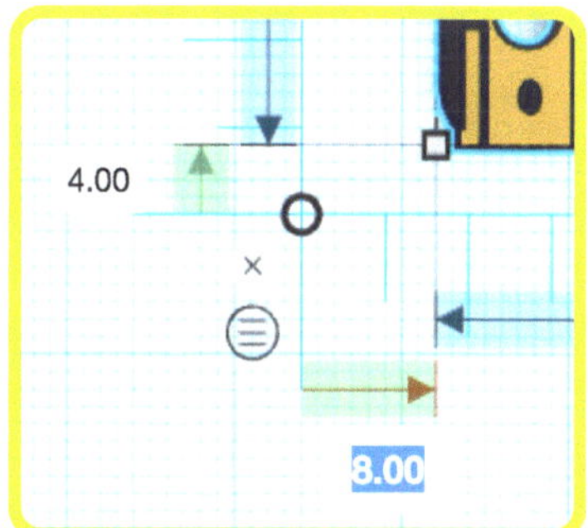

Measure It 

With the Ruler placed and the Micro:bit selected, press the circle with 3 lines by the origin. This toggles the measurement from the **endpoint** to the **midpoint** of the object. Press **X** to close the Ruler.

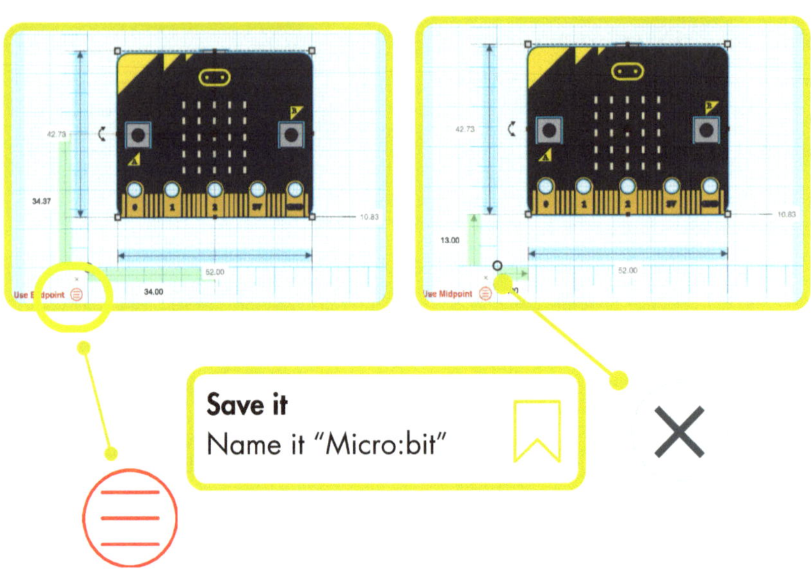

Save it
Name it "Micro:bit"

DO NOW

1. Start a new 3D Design.
2. Find the 9V battery and drag it in.

12

CHALLENGE

Measure its length, width, and height (to the top of the longest contact). Find the volume.

Scribble

The Scribble tool is your freestyle friend! Use it to break out of the polygon-based world of Basic Shapes and design something organic!

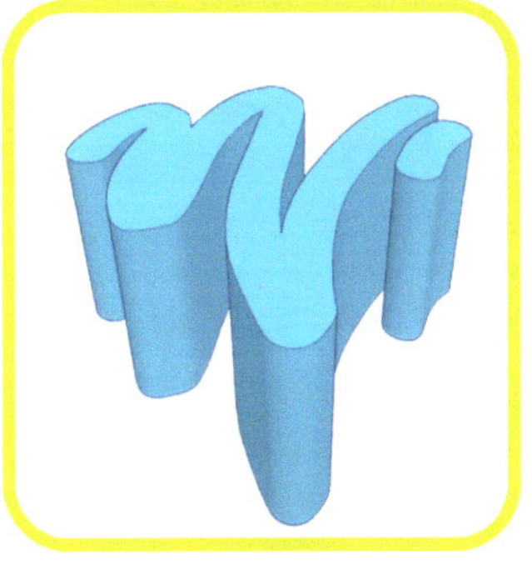

DO NOW

Find the **Scribble** button from the Basic Shapes library.

Click the Scribble button and notice the new interface.

PLAY

Try to write out a famous phrase in cursive writing.
Press the X in the preview window to close it and place the design on the Workplane.

Q: Is there a shortcut key for Scribble? Y or N

PLAY

Do a little research, why is this   phrase famous?

....

....

Scribble

Double click on the scribble design to reopen and edit it.

Use the **Erase** tool to get rid of parts of your design.

13

CHALLENGE

Find "boy standing, arms down."

Use the Scribble tool to design him some crazy hair.

PLAY

It can be tricky to Align a Scribble, so you may need to use the **Align** tool to place the hair on the head.

Q: Can a Scribble be used as a hole? Y or N

Save it
Name it "Scribble Hair"

Paste It 📋

Not only can you duplicate shapes inside a design, but you can also copy and paste them between 2 browser tabs. Open Tinkercad in 2 tabs. In one open and Copy any design, then move to the second tab, and Paste it in.

Example:

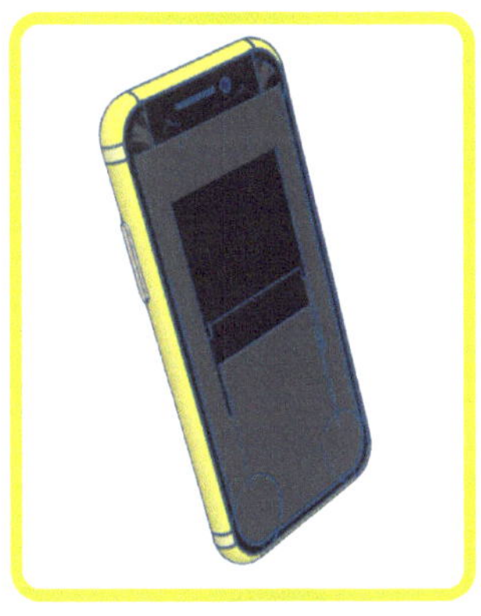

Design A
(**Copy** this: Ctrl+C)

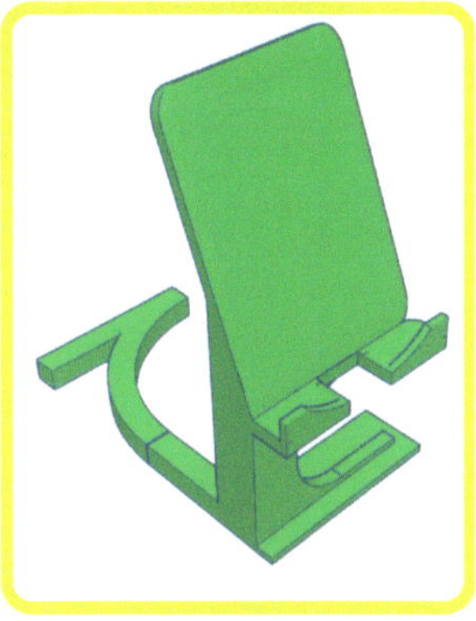

Design B
(**Paste** A into this: Ctrl+V)

Design A *in* Design B

Paste It

Search the gallery for "CADclass RACKET" and in a different tab for "CADclass DIN". **Copy and Tinker** with both of them.

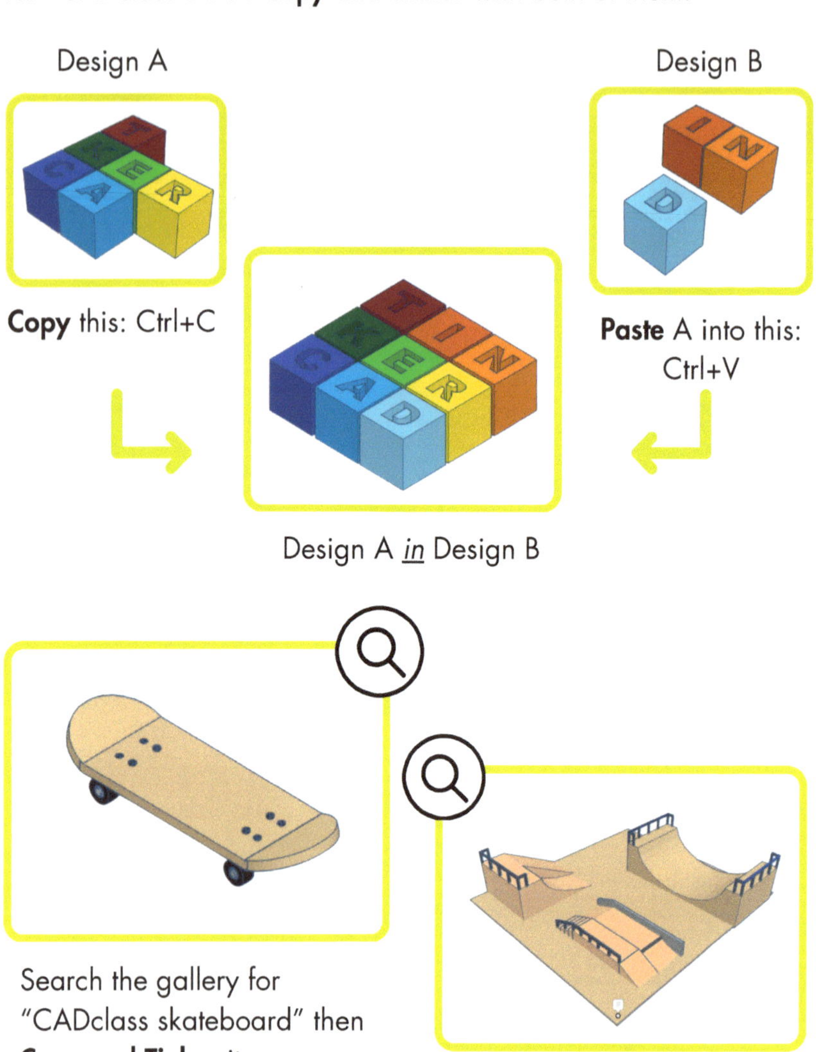

Search the gallery for "CADclass skateboard" then **Copy and Tinker** it.

In another tab search the gallery for "CADclass skate park" then **Copy and Tinker** it.

14

CHALLENGE

Combine 'CADclass skateboard' and 'CADclass skate park' into a new design. Resize and position the board on a ramp.

Save it
Name it "Skate Park"

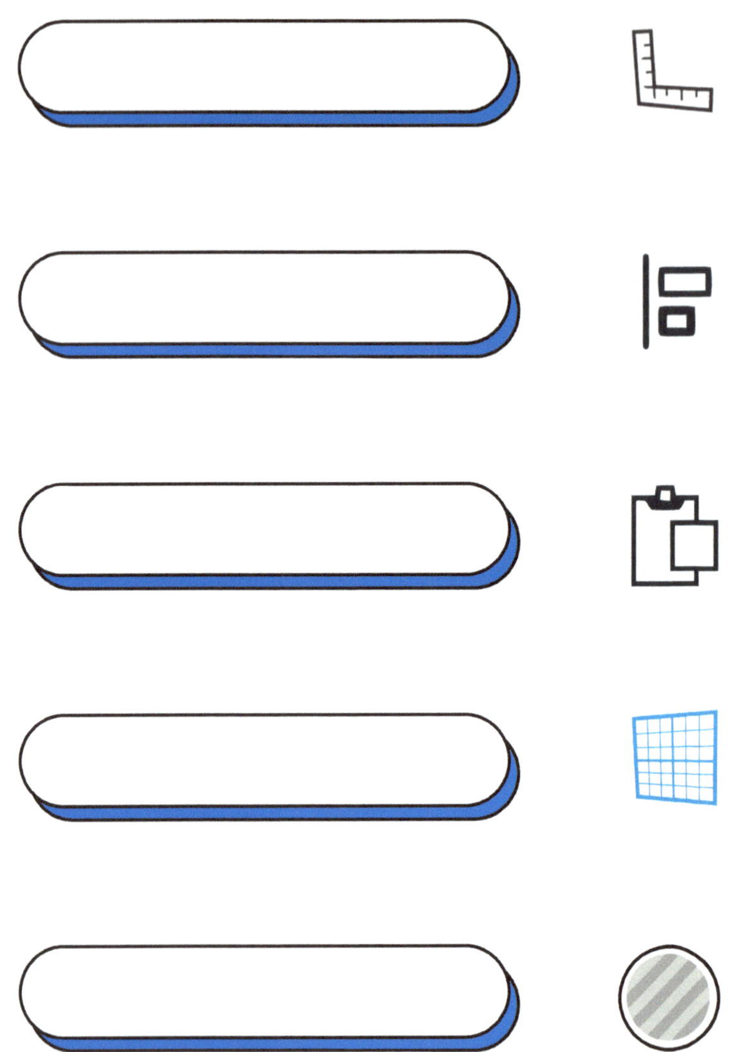

Solutions

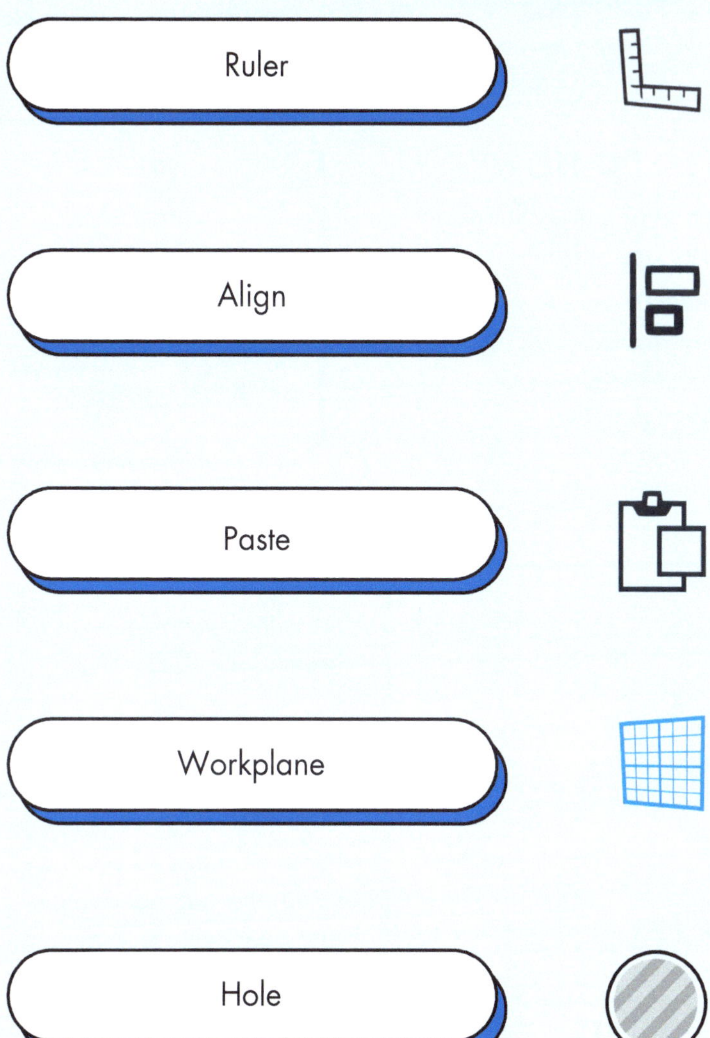

Import

3D Designs you find online are likely in STL or OBJ format. These are common types of 3D design files, like MP4 or WAV for music. You can Import these into Tinkercad to use or modify them.

DO NOW

Visit one of these 3D design repositories and find and save a "3DBenchy" STL or OBJ :

printables.com
thingiverse.com
thangs.com

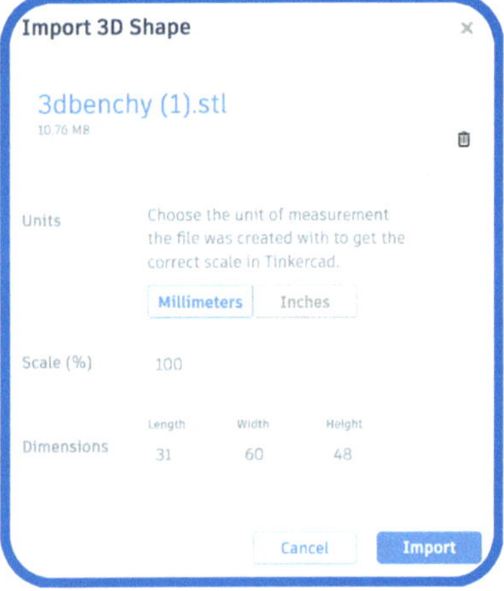

PLAY

Press the **Import** button and import your 3DBenchy.

When you import you can match the original designs units and alter scale and dimensions.

Import

2D vector graphics are common, often free online, and fun to play with in Tinkercad. You can Import and use them in many ways.

DO NOW

Visit svgrepo.com, or another source of Scalable Vector Graphics (SVG) files.

Find and save a solid SVG of an animal, and **Import** it.

Scale if necessary.

PLAY

Click on the shape and change these settings using the Dialogue Box:

1. **Fill mode** to > **Outer Line.**
2. **Corners > Rounded.**
3. **Line Width** > 3.0 mm.

You have a cookie cutter!

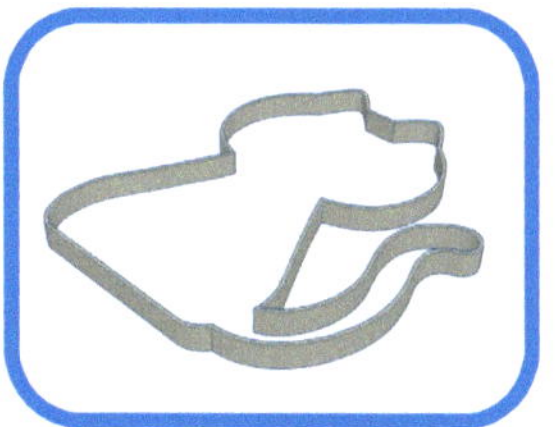

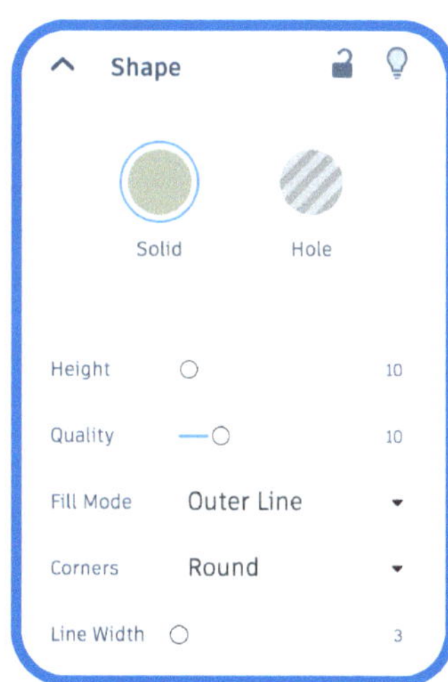

Save it
Name it "Cookie Cutter"

Laser Cut 

Laser cutters work like knives, slicing materials such as wood and plastic using focused light. You can use Tinkercad to generate SVG files that can be used as a path for a laser cutter.

An SVG is the generated profile where a design intersects (goes through) the **Workplane.** All you need to do is press **Export** and select **SVG.**

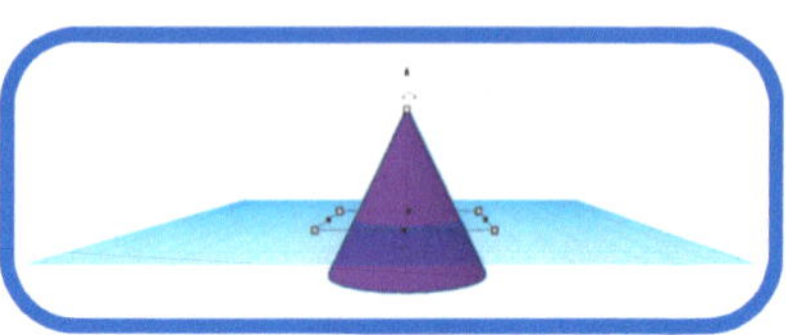

Export	.SVG

PLAY

Find an object that changes profile along its Z axis (e.g. a one, snowman, or a mountain).

Move the shape   so it intersects the **Workplane,** press **Export**, and then **SVG.**

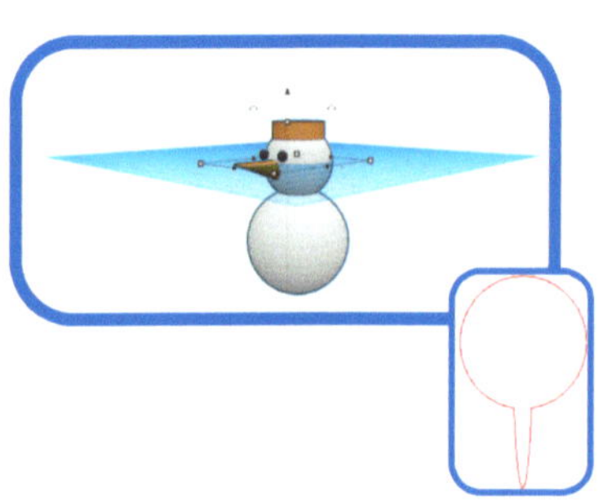

Move the shape and repeat the steps above.

Go to: <u>t.ly/HMzxO</u> to view your SVGs.

Laser Cut 

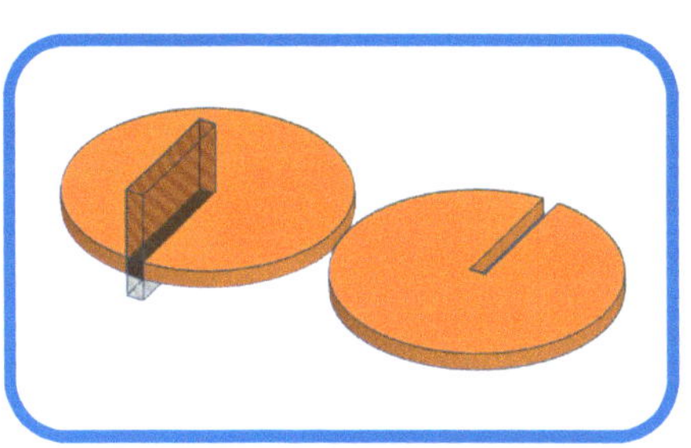

Save it
Name it "Snowflake"

OBJ | STL | SVG

2D   **3D**

Solutions 

File type	Advantages	Limitations	Uses
STL	Will produce an accurate model. Small file size. Universally used.	Limited capabilities in storing color and texture data.	Sharing 3D printable files.
OBJ	Stores surface geometry, color, and texture information. Open source.	Does not encode scene information such as light, position, or animations.	CAD, and 3D printing.
SVG	Can be scaled to any dimension without losing quality. Can be edited using JavaScript or CSS.	Only works with 2 dimensional images.	2D graphics, charts, and illustrations on websites.

Most designs from a repository will have a **Creative Commons** license attached.

Creative Commons licenses are special permissions for sharing things. They tell others how they can use the work – whether they can share it, change it, or use it commercially – without asking for permission each time. It's a way for creators to make their work available while still keeping some control over how it's used.

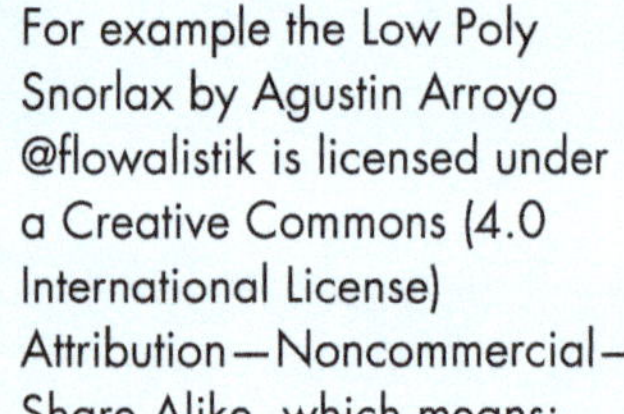

For example the Low Poly Snorlax by Agustin Arroyo @flowalistik is licensed under a Creative Commons (4.0 International License) Attribution – Noncommercial – Share Alike, which means:

✗ | Sharing without attribution
✓ | Remix Culture allowed
✗ | Commercial Use
✗ | Free Cultural Works
✗ | Meets Open Definition

t.ly/RyMu4

Solutions 

The "battle of the units" has been a long and winding journey. The imperial system traces its roots back to ancient Rome, evolving as it spread through the British Empire. The metric system originated in revolutionary France in the late 18th century.

Fast forward to the 20th century, and we find ourselves amid a glacial global measurement showdown. The metric system gained momentum internationally due to its simplicity and decimal nature. In 1960, the International System of Units (SI) was established, embracing the metric system as its foundation.

On the other hand, the imperial system, with its quirky mix of units like inches, feet, and pounds, maintains a stronghold, especially in the United States. Despite the global push towards metrication, these 2 systems coexist to this day, causing occasional confusion and unit conversion headaches. Each system has its strengths and weaknesses, and the debate over which is superior continues to echo through classrooms, laboratories, and kitchens worldwide.

Read more: Exactly: How Precision Engineers Created the Modern World by Simon Winchester t.ly/ITVR4

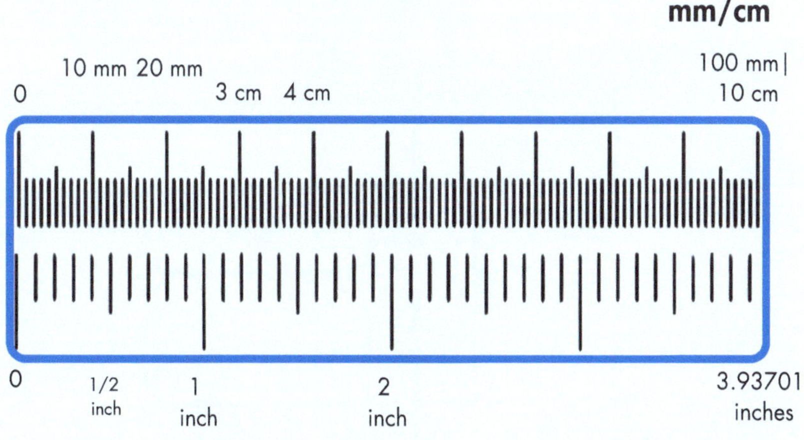

Solutions

Laser cutting is a sophisticated manufacturing process that utilizes a focused laser beam to cut through various materials, offering precision and versatility in creating intricate shapes. This technology has widespread use in the automotive and electronics industries and is particularly popular in crafting prototypes and mass-producing components. It typically cuts or engraves sheet materials.

Advantages:

Precision: Allows for intricate designs with high repeatable accuracy.

Versatility: Applicable to a variety of materials e.g. Acrylic, plywood, cardboard, and more.

Speed and Efficiency: Faster than traditional cutting methods, reducing production time.

Minimal Waste: Optimizes material usage for sustainability.

Limitations:

Material Thickness: Less effective for extremely thick materials.

Initial Cost: Expensive equipment may be a barrier for small businesses.

Material Limits: Not suitable for all materials due to fumes or compatibility e.g. it can engrave, but not cut metals

Skill Requirement: Trained technicians needed for setup and programming.

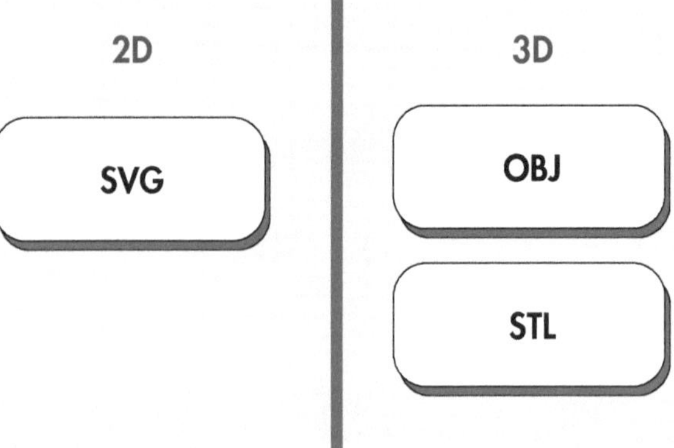

Solutions

Not all laser cutter CAM software will accept SVG format, so you may need to convert it: convertio.co/svg-png/

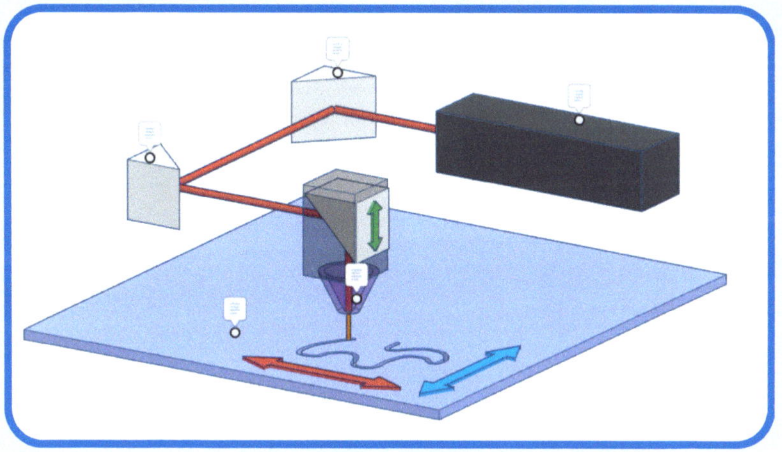

CADclass CNC laser cutter
t.ly/DgONm

Export & 3D Print

3D printers make real objects from digital designs. Most 3D printers use a heated extruder that melts plastic filament and builds up the model layer by layer. It's a magic machine that creates something from nothing!

DO NOW

Open your brick design.

Navigate to and press **Export** then **STL**.

Export

.STL

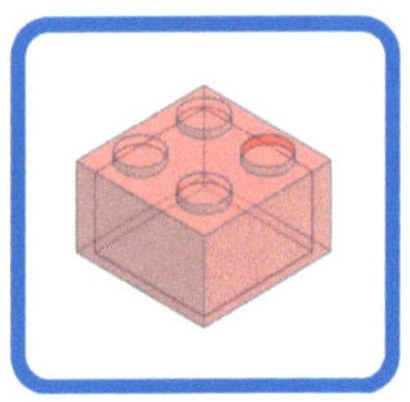

The 3D model starts as a digital Tinkercad design. It's then exported as an STL or OBJ.

The STL is cut into layers in a slicer program. These layers are converted into G-code, a language that a 3D printer can understand.

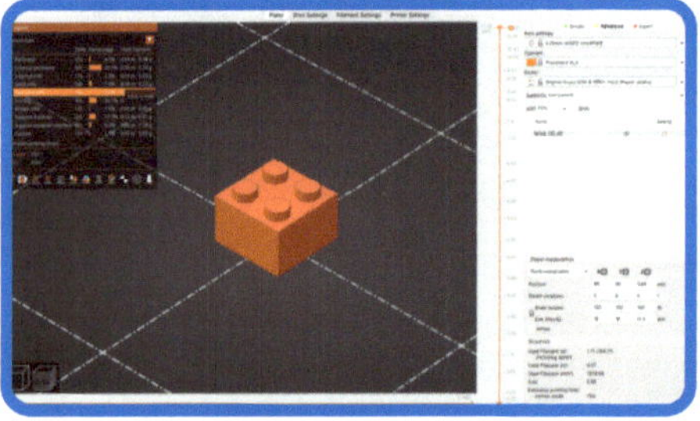

Filament and the G-code are fed into the machine where your model will come into reality!

Export & Send

Tinkercad lets you easily Export or Send To your design to use in another program in many different ways.

| Export | Send To |

DO NOW

Open any of your saved designs and find and press the **Export** and **Send To** buttons. Explore the options.

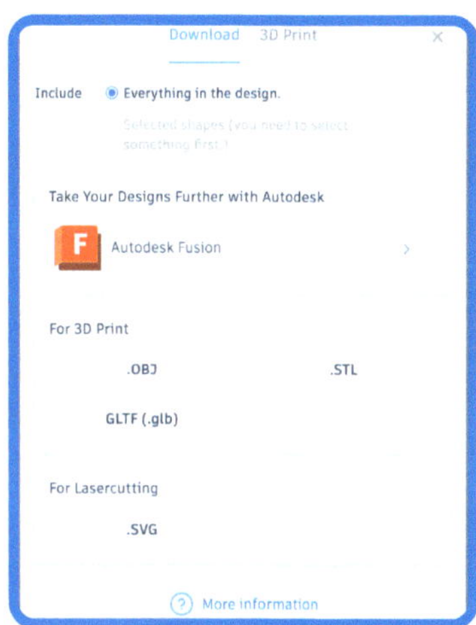

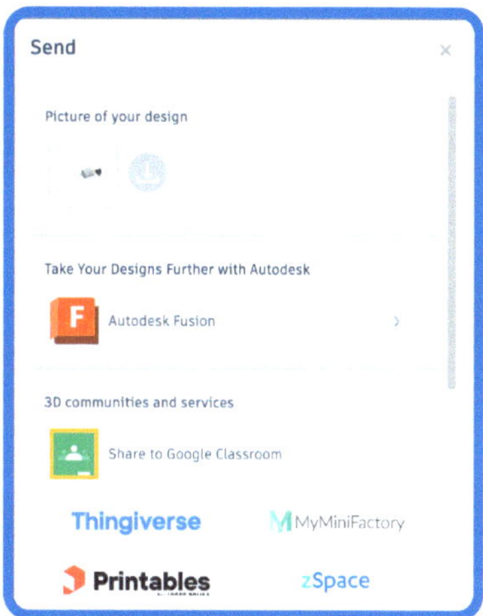

Check the 4 file types you can Export:

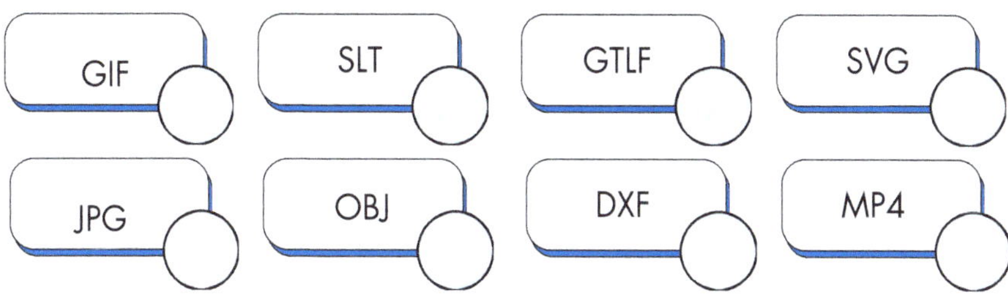

Export & Send 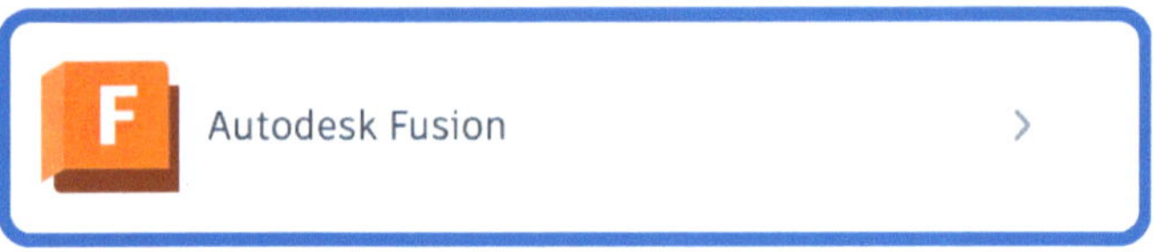

Tinkercad is made by Autodesk. Its big brother, Fusion, is more powerful and has many customization options.

One of the Export links is called Send to Fusion, which sends your Tinkercad design straight to Fusion if you already have it installed and open.

If you are interested in learning Fusion, use this link to find out more

The Ultimate Online Fusion
CAD Class
CADclass.org

There are also many new AI-powered rendering tools (used to make digital designs more realistic). If you are interested, search for and try one with one of your Tinkercad creations.

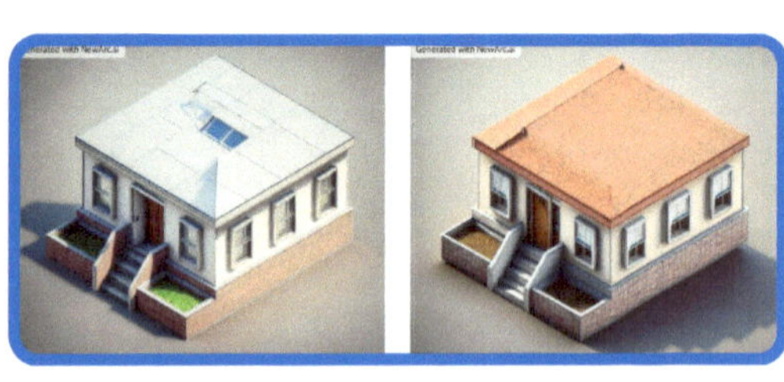

Workspace Setup 

Switch up the visual vibe of your Tinkercad workspace by pressing the Settings button to customize the look and feel!

DO NOW

Start a new 3D Design.

Find and press the **Settings** button located near the bottom right of the screen.

Settings

Explore the options.

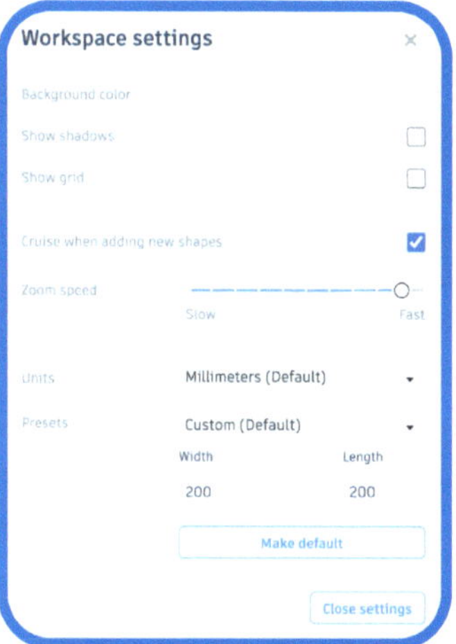

Q: How many preset background colors are there?

255   21   12   36

PLAY

Find and press the **Presets** dropdown arrow.

Q: What do all the names in the presets refer to?
A: 3D Printers B: File types

Makerbot Replicator Z18

Makerbot Replicator 2

Type A Machines Series 1

Ultimaker Original+

Ultimaker 2+

Ultimaker 2 Go

Ultimaker 3

16

CHALLENGE

Design a boat and make the workplane a narrow river and the background a dark night.

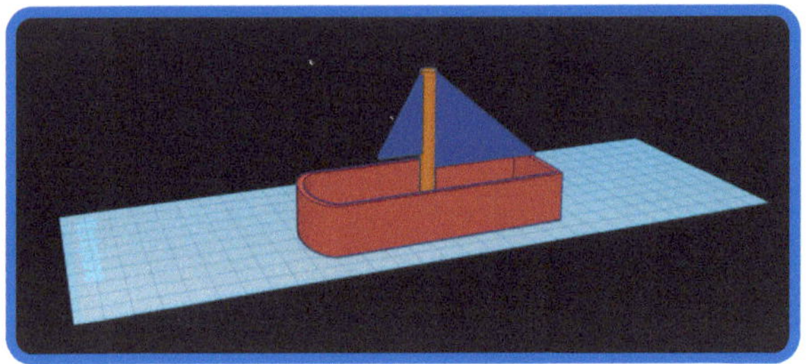

PLAY

"**Make Default**" sets your next new designs **Workplane** to that size automatically. If you have a 3D printer or laser cutter, you could set the default to those bed dimensions.

PLAY

How else could you make the appearance of water for the river? ( look at Hide It)

Save it
Name it "Night Boat"

Solutions 

Changing the workspace setup defaults in CAD software is essential because every designer has their preferred way of working. Allowing users to customize the workspace helps them create an environment that suits their workflow, making them more comfortable and efficient. For example, a dark background can reduce eye strain, and your country may use units different from the default.

Depending on which browser you are using, additional accessibility options are available. In Chrome, go to the top-right corner of the browser window and click on the 3 vertical dots to open the menu. Hover over Settings and click on Appearance. You can change the font, font size, page zoom, and more here. You can also visit the Chrome web store for more Accessibility Apps: t.ly/wevUy

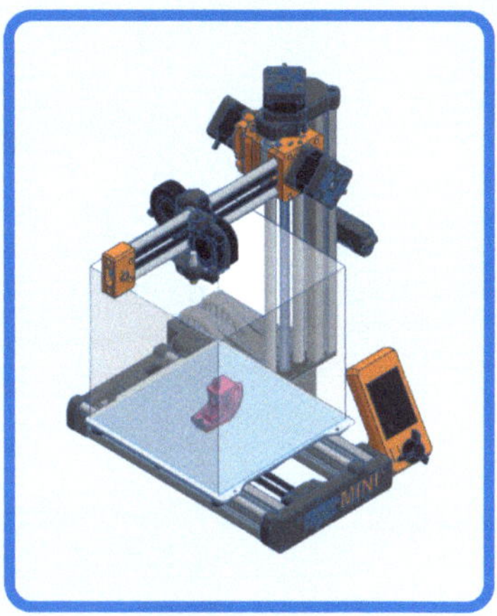

In this example the original creator juliencasimir83 has recreated a Prusa Mini 3D printer so that the print-bed (the surface used to build the design on) is the same size as the Tinkercad Workplane 7"×7" (18×18 cm).

This visual scaffolding can help learners make the link between the CAD they are designing in, and the machine they could make it with.

All the names in the presets refer to types of 3D printers - some look very old now (look up "Type A Machines Series 1") or watch this: t.ly/W52ax

A: There are 36 preset background colors.

Prusa Mini
t.ly/mp6lB

Custom Shapes 

Sometimes you'll want to make and/or save a shape that doesn't exist. The more custom shapes you save, the more complex your custom designs can be.

Shape Generators

Find and select the **Shape Generators** button at the bottom of the parts library list.

PLAY

Find the "Pointed Windmill Blade" and select it.

Play with the variables!

How to Design the Best Wind Farm Blade in Tinkercad
t.ly/PFGB-

Custom Shapes

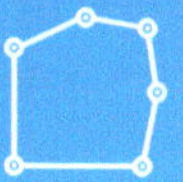

Want something more specific? You'll need to create your own Custom Shape, which only takes a few simple steps. Begin by opening a new 3D Design to make a building brick.

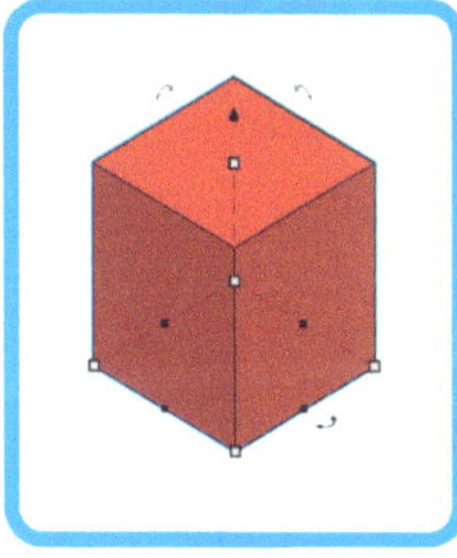

1. Add and resize a Box to 8.0 x 8.0 x 9.6 mm.

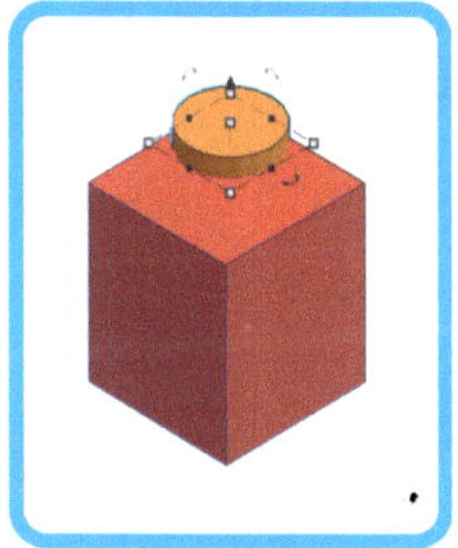

2. **Cruise** a Cylinder onto the top face and make it 4.8 x. 4.8 x 1.7 mm.

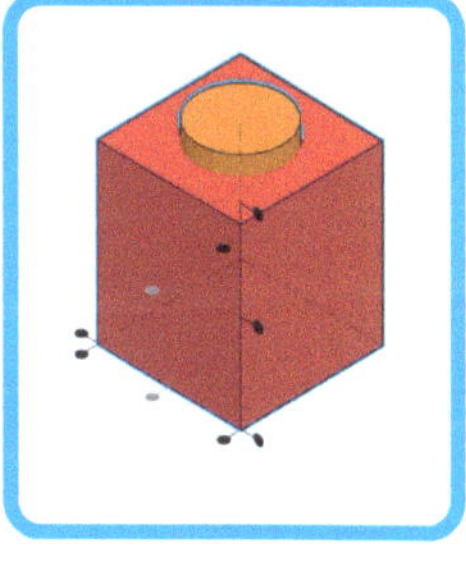

3. **Align** then **Group** them together.

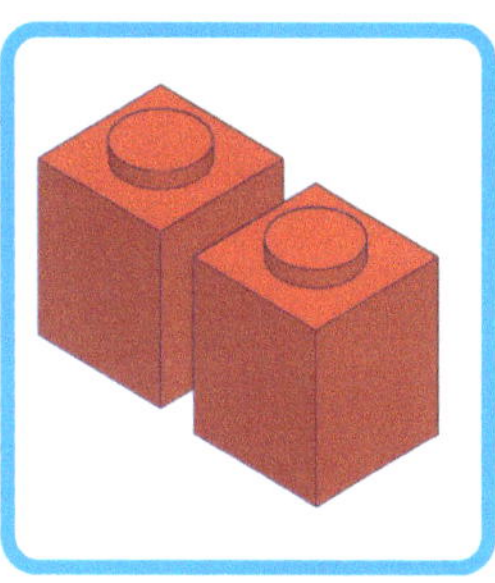

4. Make a **Copy**.

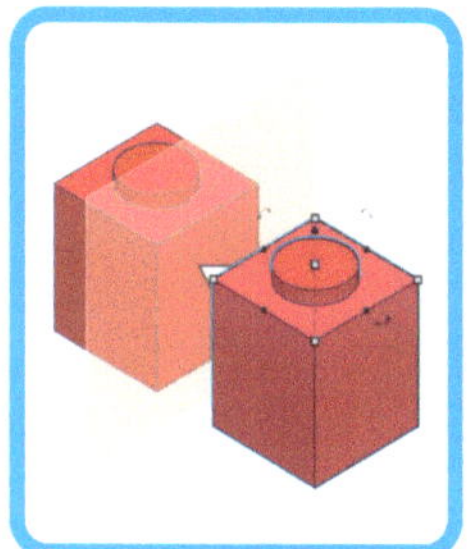

5. Create a **Workplane**, place it on the side of the original and drop **(D)** the **Copy** onto it. **Align** them.

6. Make this a **Group**, **Copy** & **Paste** it, and **Align** it.

HINT: look at the Workplanes chapter for help.

Custom Shapes 

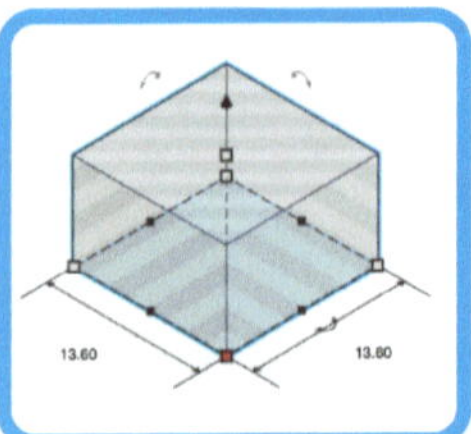

7. Add a new Box, make it 13.8 x 13.8 x 8.4 mm, and set it to be a Hole.

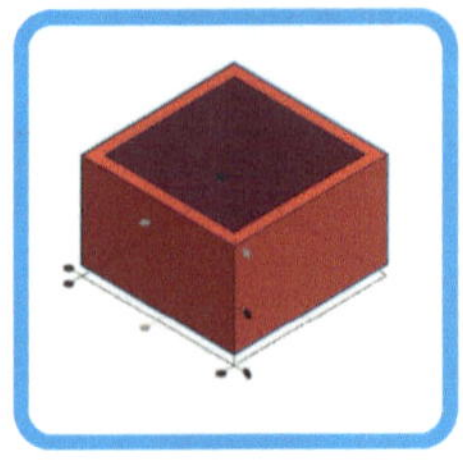

8. **Align** and **Group** to hollow out the solid.

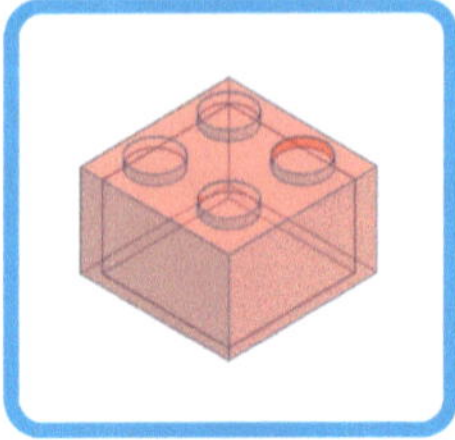

9. Change the color, or make it **transparent** so you can see the internal details.

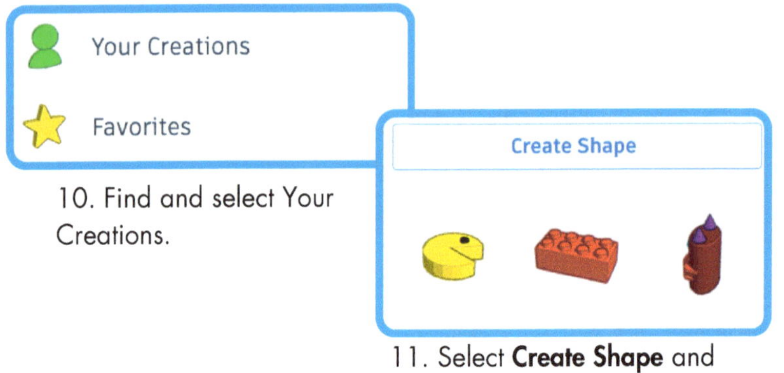

10. Find and select Your Creations.

11. Select **Create Shape** and click on your shape.

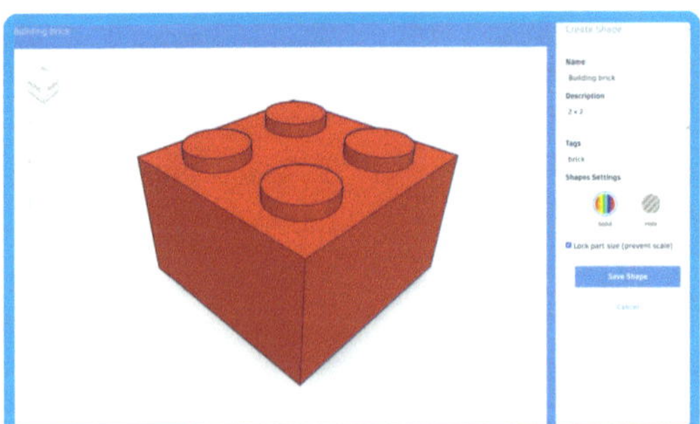

12. Give it a name, description, add tags, and lock the part size. Save it!

Save Shape

Solutions

3D printing, like paper printing, is seemingly simple. However, there are many steps to get your machine set up properly and many things that can go wrong! Here's a basic 3D printing workflow overview:

Prepare the File: Before printing the object, you must prepare the STL file using slicing software, such as Cura or PrusaSlicer. This software takes the 3D model and slices it into thin layers, which the printer can then build up.

Import the STL: Open the slicing software and import the STL file. To customize the print, you can adjust settings like layer height, infill density, and print speed.

Slice the Model: Once you're happy with the settings, click Slice to generate the G-code. This set of instructions tells the printer how to move and extrude the filament to create the object.

Save the G-code: Save the G-code file to an SD card or USB drive, which you'll use to transfer the file to the printer.

Load Filament: Before you start the print, you'll need to load the filament into the printer. This involves feeding the filament through the extruder and into the hot end, where it will melt and be deposited onto the print bed.

Start the Print: Insert the SD card or USB drive into the printer and select the G-code file you want to print. The printer will then start the print, following the instructions in the G-code file to create the object layer by layer.

Remove the Object: After finishing the print, remove the object from the print bed. Be careful, as it may still be hot.

Post-Processing: Depending on the object, you may need to do some post-processing, such as removing support material, sanding rough edges, or painting the object.

Solutions 

You can do many things when designing to give yourself the best chance of success. Here are some useful links:

From our friends at Printlab: Designing for 3D Printing
t.ly/R-MYe

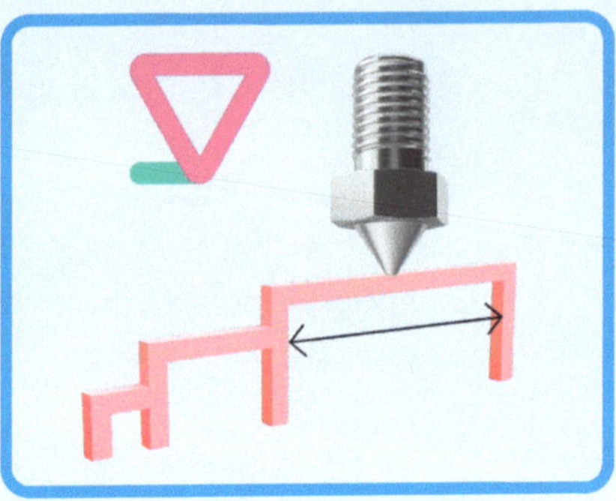

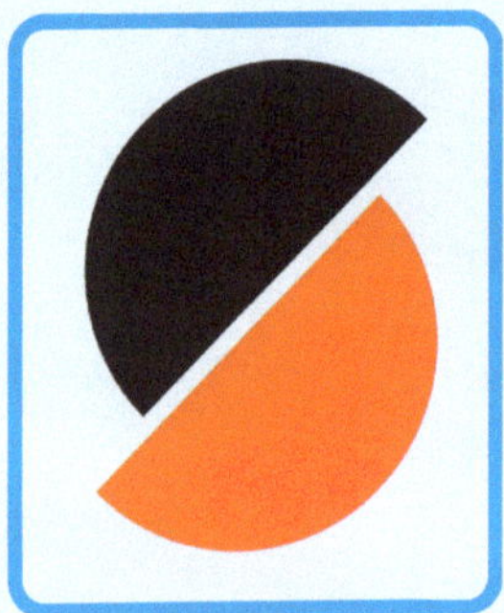

PrusaSlicer: Slice with style! The Beginner's Guide
t.ly/haZ7v

Cura: Setup to success 3D printing guide
t.ly/GRQd9

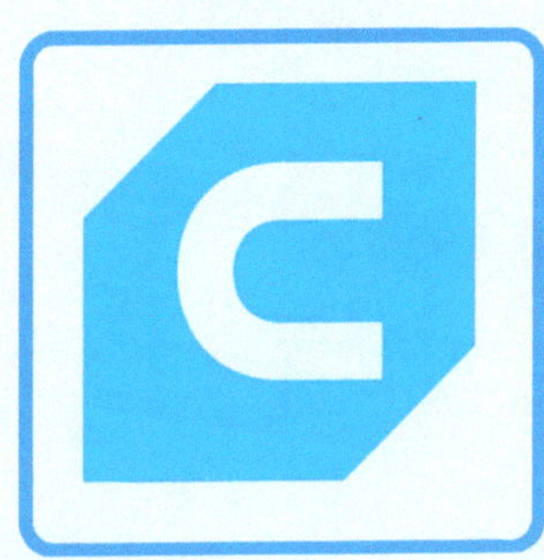

Solutions 

CAD and CAM unite design and manufacturing, allowing you to translate ideas in your head to ideas on a computer and ideas on the computer to an automated machine that makes real-world stuff.

CAD is the Engineer, Architect, or Designer responsible for creating 3D drawings of imagined ideas. Since you're working through this book, you should now understand this.

CAM (Computer-Aided Manufacturing) is a set of instructions that tells the machines what to do based on 2D or 3D objects. In 3D printing, for example, your machine must know how much material to extrude, how fast the Hot End moves, how much plastic the inside of your model has, and many other things. Like coding, these machines require precise step-by-step instructions to work. Fortunately, CAM software simplifies most of these instructions, allowing you to focus on the desired outcome instead of how to write each instruction (line of G-code).

You will know if you have ever used Word or Google Docs (a type of CAD) that getting CAM (an inkjet printer) to make it can be problematic. Things can get tricky when you want to use a particular type of paper or change a default setting. You can learn a lot more about CAM using Cura at CADclass.org/courses/cura

Some 3D printing design guidelines:

- Avoid overhangs and wide bridges.
- Don't make the walls too thin.
- Maximize the flat area on the print-bed - reorient if necessary.
- Add fillets and chamfers to sharp edges if you can.
- Avoid sharp and narrow points.

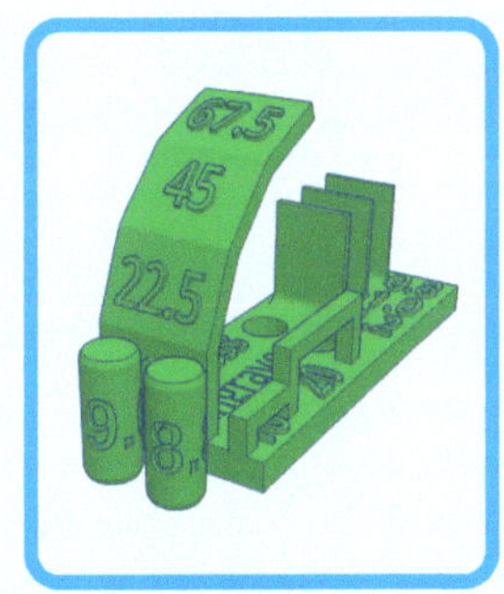

Get to know your printer - find out what it can and cannot do using a design like "FFF Print Rules Block" by Sam Booth t.ly/Yv3XU

Solutions 

Check the 4 file types you can Export:

GIF ⚪	SLT ✅	GTLF ✅	SVG ✅
JPG ⚪	OBJ ✅	DXF ⚪	MP4 ⚪

3D Printing Masterclass:
Ender 3 Assembly &
Fundamentals
t.ly/8qVtZ

True or False?

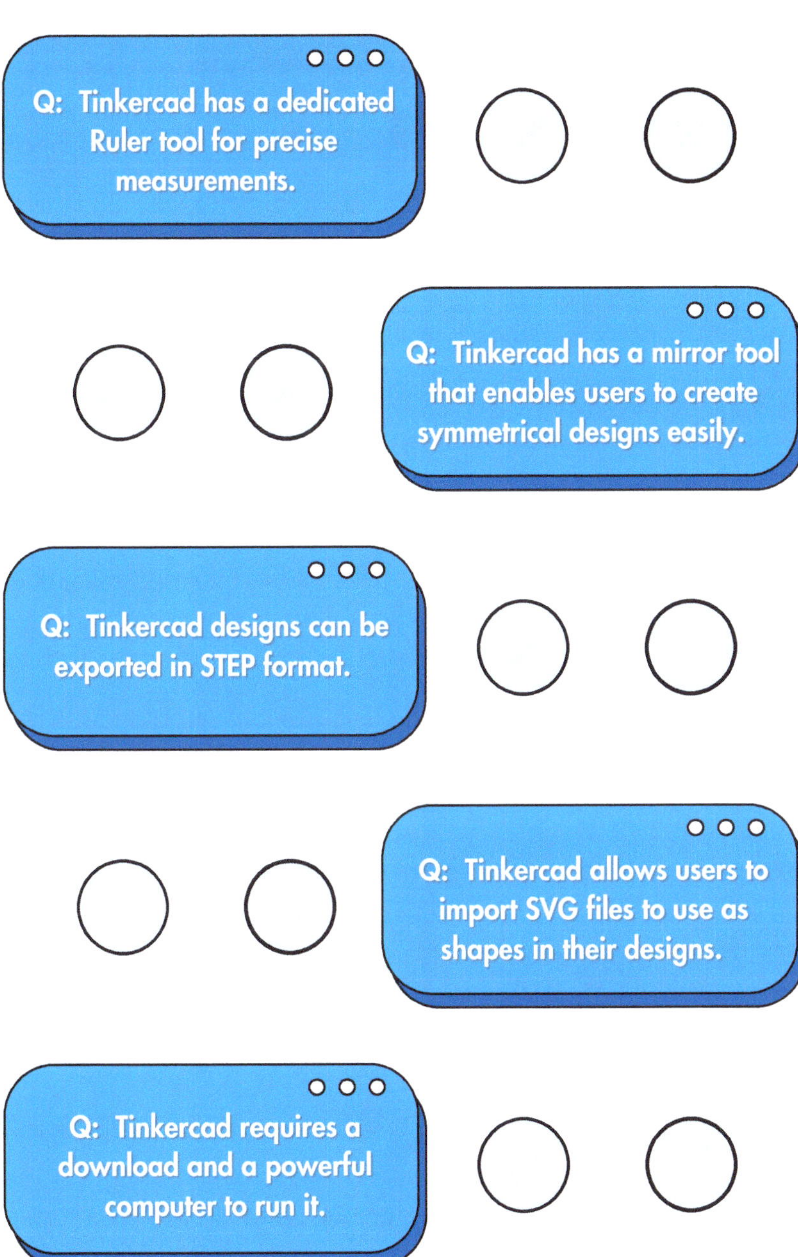

Solutions 

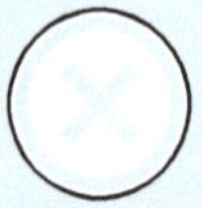

Q: Tinkercad has a dedicated Ruler tool for precise measurements.

A: Yes, it has a Ruler tool

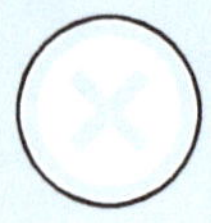

A: Yes, it has a Mirror tool (M)

Q: Tinkercad has a mirror tool that enables users to create symmetrical designs easily.

Q: Tinkercad designs can be exported in STEP format.

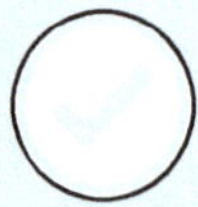

A: You can olny export STL and OBJ and GTFL files

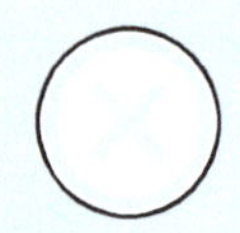

A: Yes, and also OBJ and SVG

Q: Tinkercad allows users to import SVG files to use as shapes in their designs.

Q: Tinkercad requires a download and a powerful computer to run it.

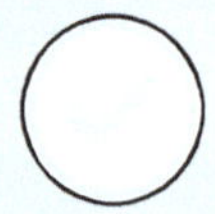

A: It runs in any modern browser. An app is suggested, but not mandatory on an iPad.

Add Notes

Notes are a great way to leave messages for yourself and others. You'll find the Notes button above the Shapes menu, next to the Ruler and Workplane icons, or use the keyboard shortcut N.

DO NOW

Search the gallery and find a model of the solar system.

Use the **Notes** tool to label the planets.

17

CHALLENGE

Find a model of a bicycle and label all its mechanisms e.g. chain, lever, bearing...

The Bicycle by Bartosz Ciechanowski
https://t.ly/PFGB-

Solutions 

Ways you can use **Notes**:

Ask students to annotate their designs

1. Identify shapes, e.g., this is Box 1.
2. Explain features they can't show, e.g., this is made from Oak.
3. Use Notes to offer feedback when assessing their work, for example, "Great work, you could try using the "SVG revolver tool" to create this shape more efficiently?"

Find "box" by user "ZDP189" and explore how he has used notes.

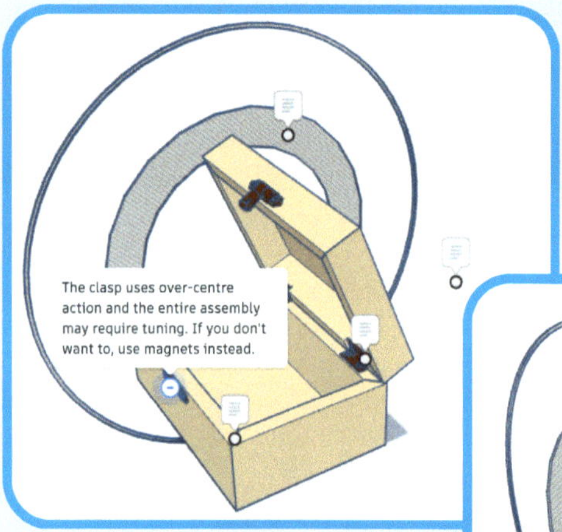

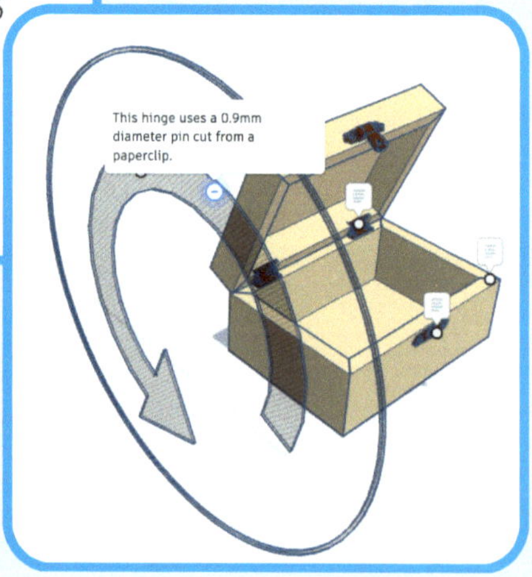

Custom Colors 

Sometimes, you'll like how Tinkercad makes things look; other times, you won't. To change your creations, you have two options: the Preset button or the Custom button!

DO NOW

Create a new shape made from many different objects.

Use the **Solid** button to make each shape a different color.

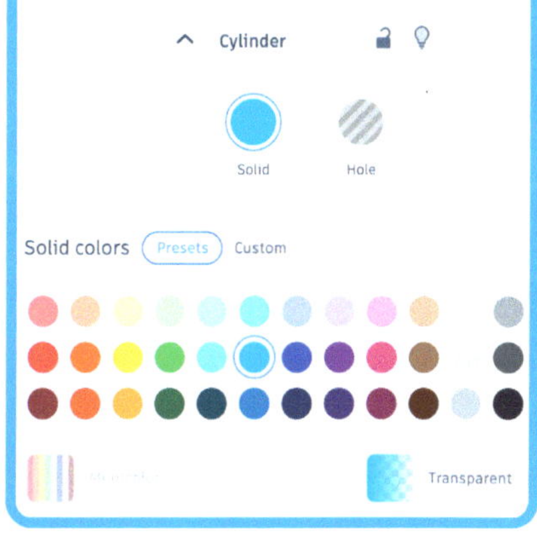

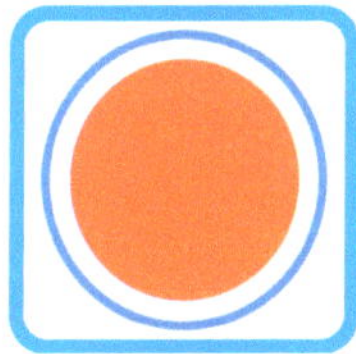

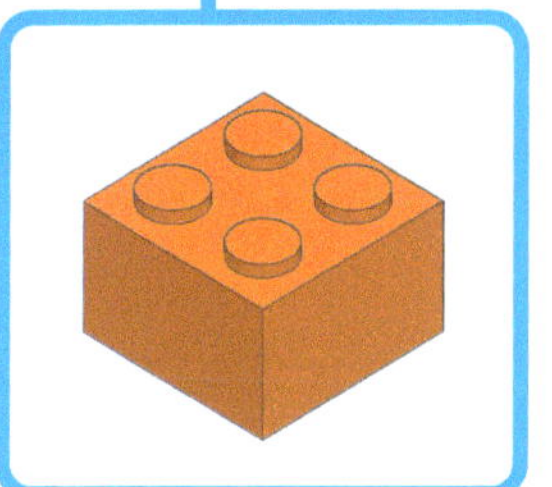

PLAY

Group it all together and notice how it changes to be a single color.

If you want every part to be a different color, press **Multicolor**.

Custom Colors 

The **Custom** button allows you to make any color you want. You can pick a color, add your own RGB or HSB, or even enter a specific Hex code.

DO NOW

Go to
encycolorpedia.com/flags

Use it to find the hex codes for a simple flag you like.

Make a note of them:

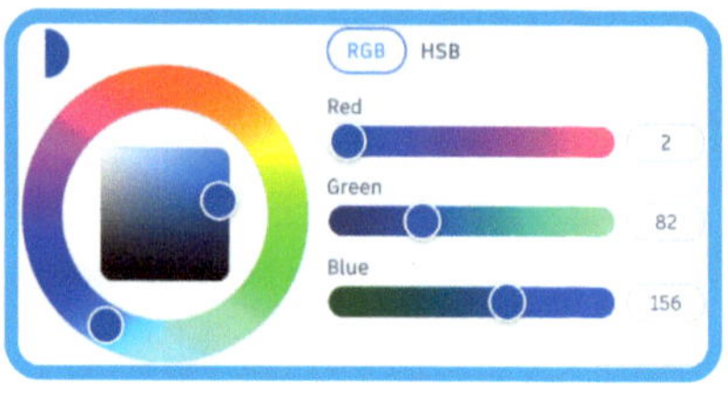

....

....

PLAY

Start a new 3D Design.
Recreate the geometry of the design.

This is the Icelandic flag geometry:

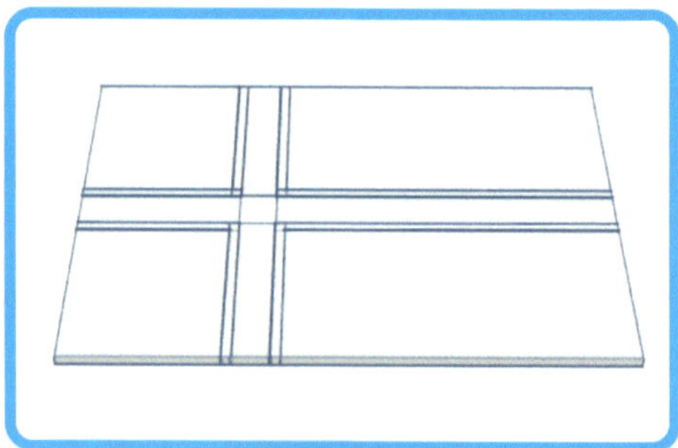

Custom Colors

For the Icelandic people, the flag's coloring represents a vision of their country's landscape. The colors stand for 3 of the elements that make up the island. Red is the fire produced by the island's volcanoes, white recalls the ice and snow that covers the land, and the blue is for the mountains of the island.
en.wikipedia.org/wiki/Flag_of_Iceland

PLAY

Select parts of the geometry, then apply the Hex or RGB codes using the **Custom** button to match the flag.

Presets Custom

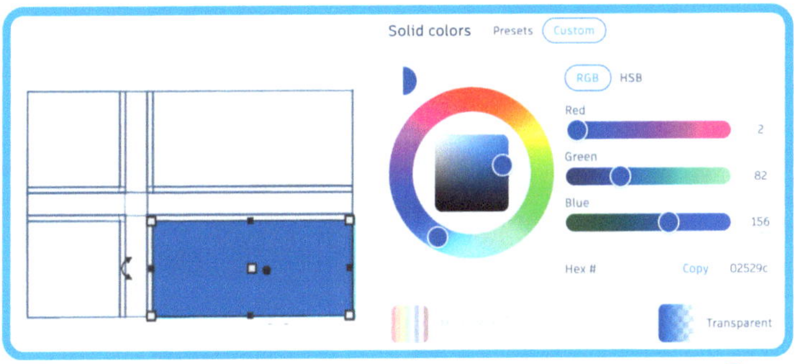

02529c

Save it
Name it "[country] Flag"

Custom Colors

Colors can also be a gradient. Do this challenge, but pay close attention, it's tricky!

CHALLENGE

Create a complex shape with a gradient color

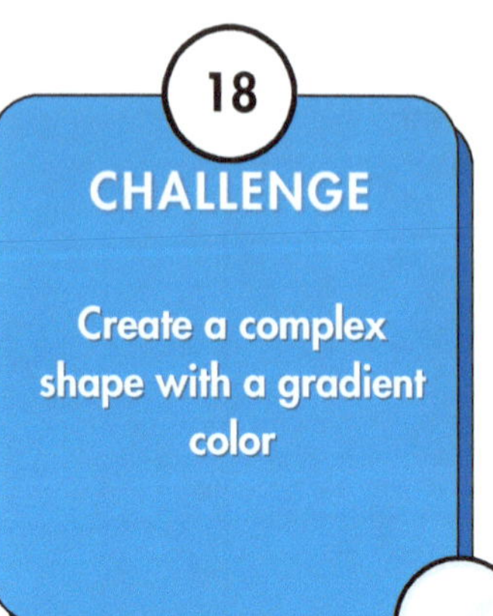

DO NOW

1. Search the gallery for a complex design like the "Aluminium Lattice Structure" by bethanytabiG9H7H and **Copy and Tinker** it.

2. Find a "gradient block" like Gradient Bumper Pack by ZDP189 and **Copy and Tinker** one of the blocks.

3. Resize the block so it's slightly bigger than the lattice. Make a **Copy** and change its color to **Solid**.

4. Set the lattice to be a **Hole, Align** it inside the solid colored shape, and then **Group** them.

5. Turn this new shape into a **Hole** and **Align** it with the gradient block.

6. **Group** them. Voila!

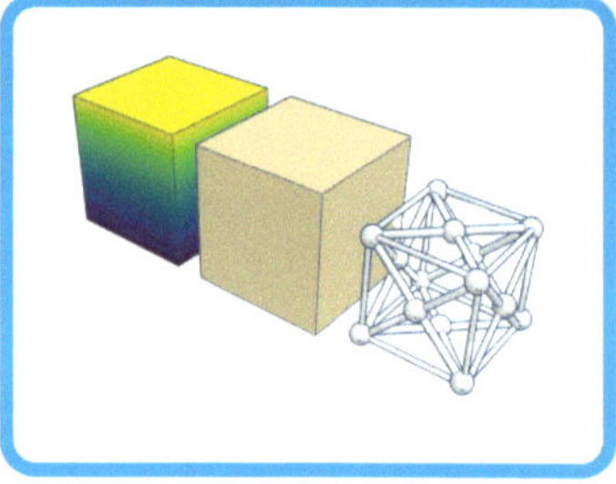

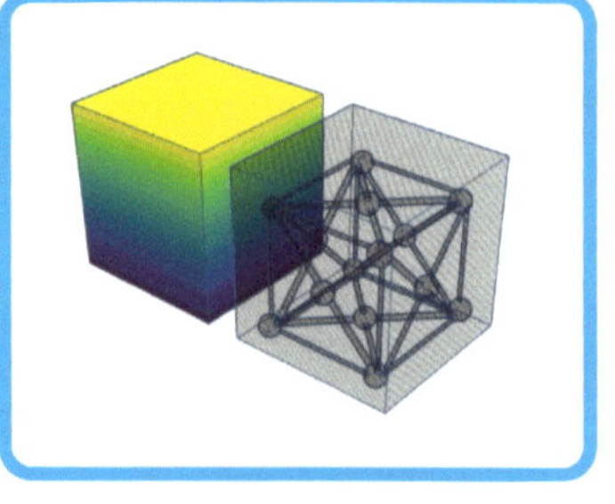

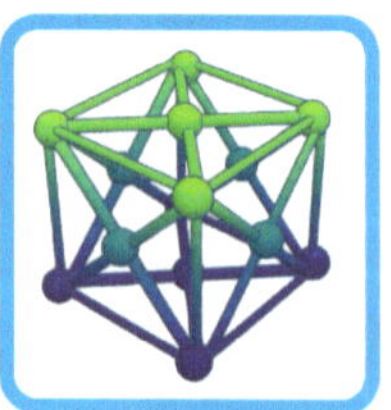

Blocks & Bricks 

Can you brick it? Yes, you can! Press the **Blocks** or **Bricks** button to transform your design into blocks or bricks.

DO NOW

Find a "Soma Cube" puzzle in the gallery. Make a **Copy** to **Tinker It**.

Press the waffle icon whenever you want to get back to the 3D design space.

PLAY

Try to re-make it in both the blocks and bricks environments. Play with the design detail buttons to alter the brick/block size.

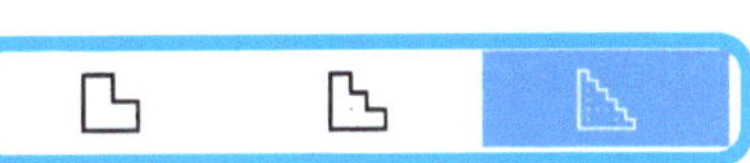

Blocks & Bricks 

Try the **Layers** button to get layer-by-layer build instructions.

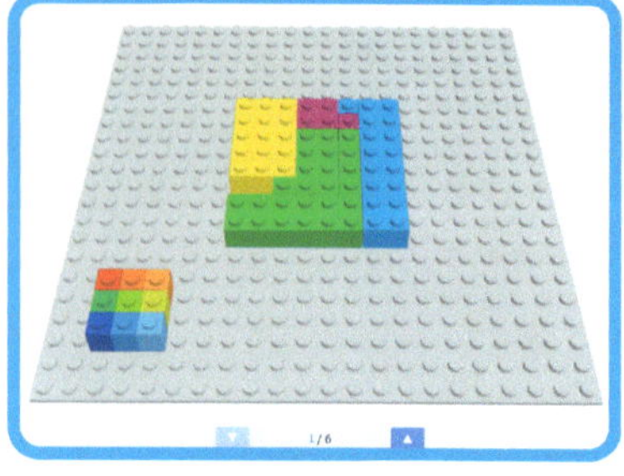

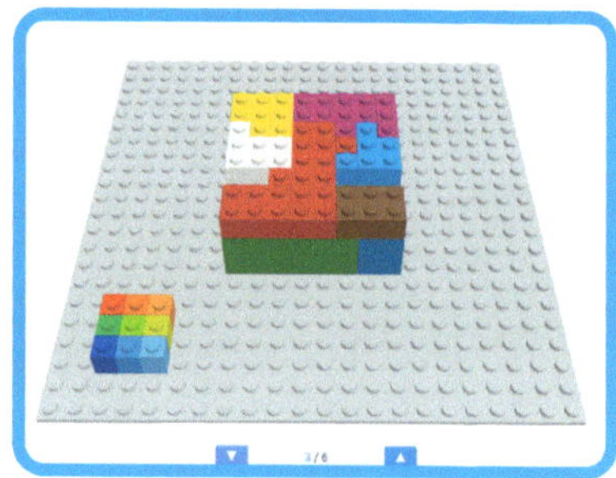

Save it
Name it "Soma Cube"

A: You can export a block's design as a schematic to load into a popular block-based digital design world.

We believe Tinkercad belongs alongside famous building block systems and digital design worlds as a titan of play and creativity.

It's a fantastic design tool limited only by the imagination.

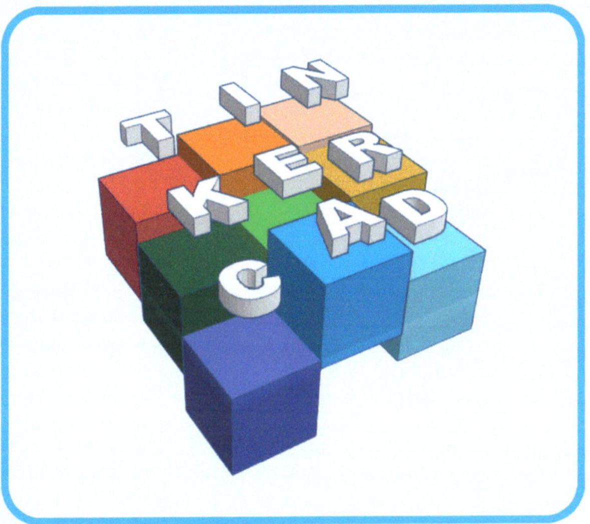

So, what problem are you going to solve today?

Collaborate 

Sharing is caring. Tap the Invite People button in the upper right corner to team up and share your work. Press Generate New Link to create a unique link. Links never expire, but the old one will stop working if you generate a new one.

Generate new link

When collaborating you'll only see the outcome of the collaborators work, not them moving their mouse or changing the view.

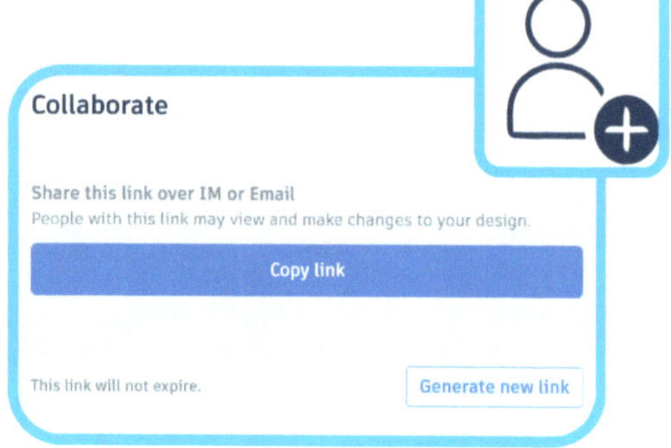

Solutions 

Collaboration is necessary to unite multiple designers, engineers, and product developers. Products like the iPhone showcase the power of collaborative creativity. Designs often go through thousands of iterations, making communication, file naming, and organization critical tasks.

As a CAD instructor, you'll want to help students understand how and when to share a file, keep track of changes, get feedback on designs, and generally stay organized. There are a variety of industry standards and unique organizational systems that make it difficult to prescribe best practices.

Here are the top 4 considerations to keep in mind:

1) Save files in predictable locations. Use Collections and folders/subfolders, like you would on Google Docs or your computer.

2) Keep naming conventions consistent. For example, Ed_cookiecutter_heart_V1 from an earlier exercise.

3) Archive completed projects that are no longer actively in use

4) Stay consistent!

More detailed descriptions here: t.ly/E8c9o

Sim Lab

The **Sim Lab** is a magical 3D playground where you can tweak gravity, switch up materials, create joints, and throw objects! Tap the falling apple icon to dive in!

PLAY

In the 3D space create an aligned see-saw / teeter-totter like this.

Then press the **Sim Lab** icon and click one of the cubes.

Press the **Material** button and select a dense material like steel.

Press the **play** button in the bottom left corner to simulate it!

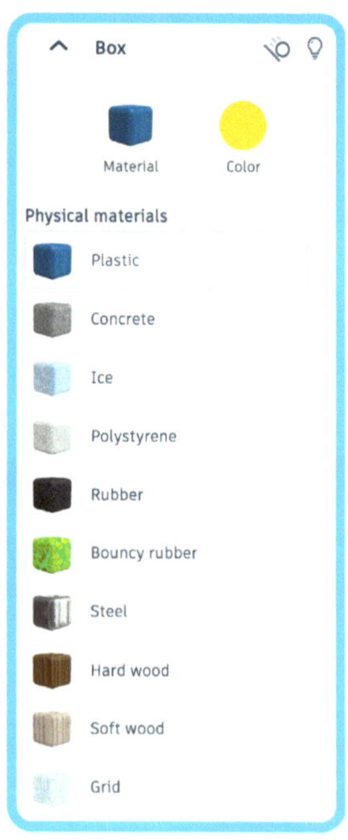

While the Sim is working press the left mouse button to throw stuff!

Press **Reset** to start over.

Sim Lab

You can add Connectors to establish relationships between parts, allowing them to turn, twist, and slide. Let's look at the Axle, which creates a wheel-and-axle relationship between parts.

DO NOW

1. Start in the 3D space and recreate this design, **Aligning** the end of the red part to the center of the Cylinder.

2. Navigate to the **Sim Lab** and place the **Axle Connector** (bottom right) on the top face of the Cylinder.

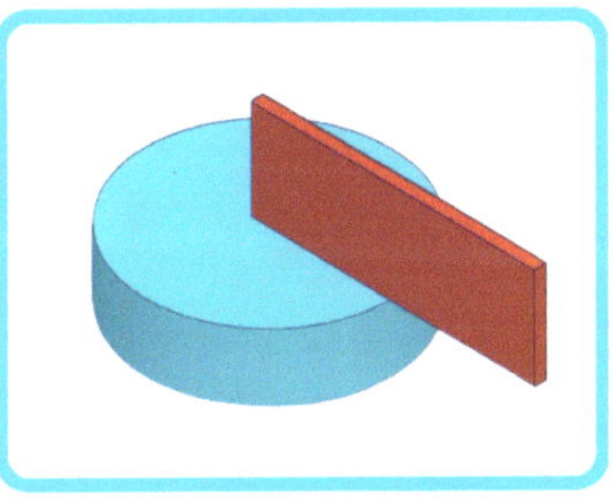

3. Go back to the 3D design space and make sure they are all **Aligned**.

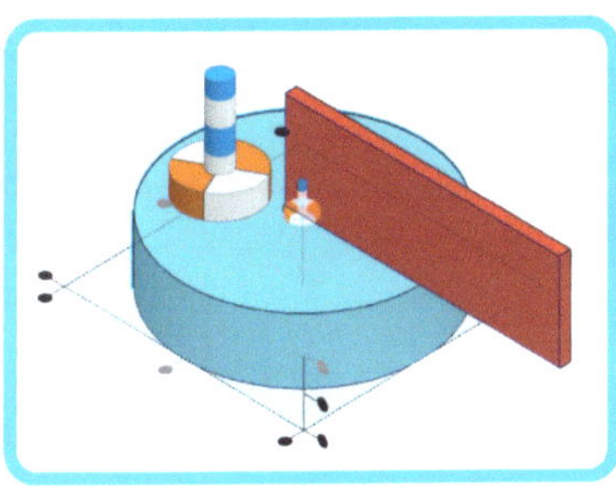

4. Select the **Axle Connector** and drag the orange/white disc on onto the red part and the blue/white disc onto the blue part.

5. Back in the Sim Lab, press **Play** and click the left mouse to throw stuff and make the paddle spin!

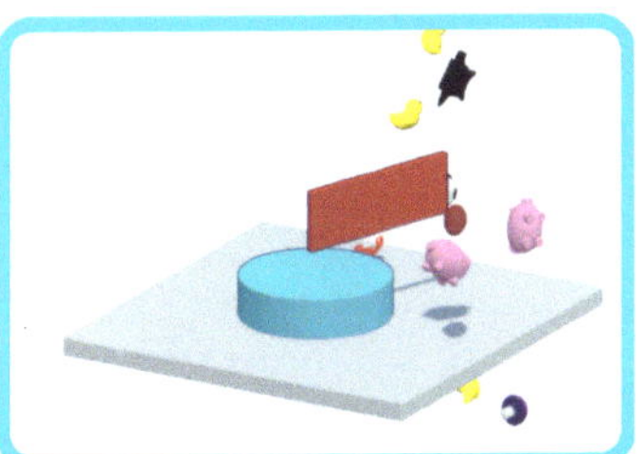

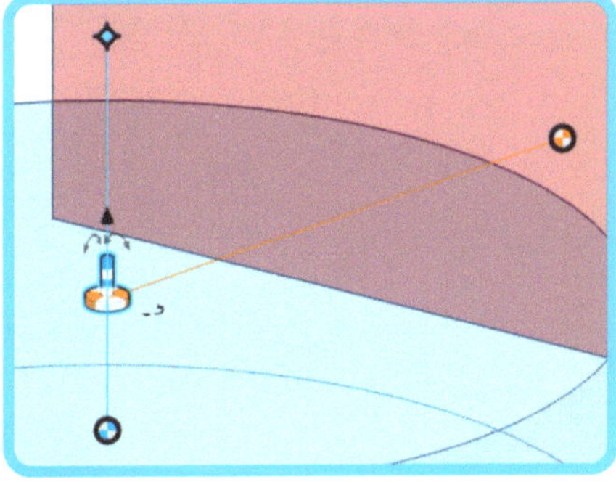

Number the Features

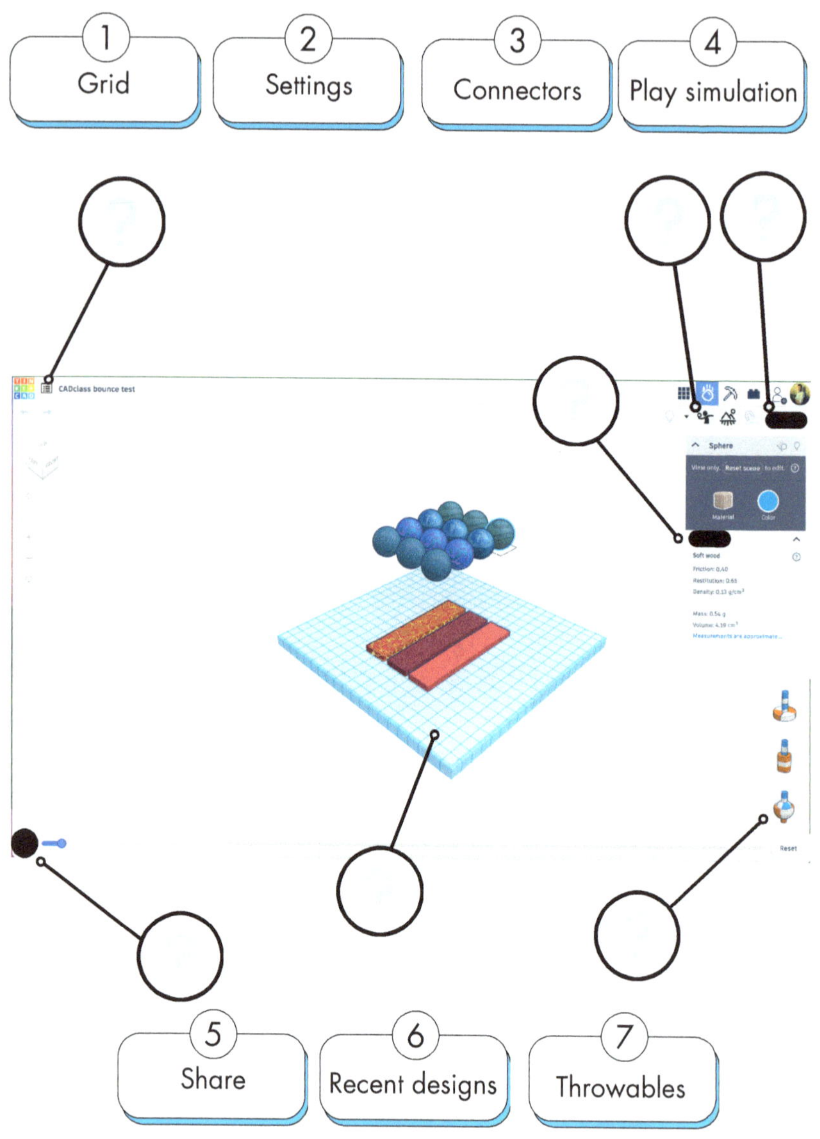

Solutions 

1. Grid
2. Settings
3. Connectors
4. Play simulation

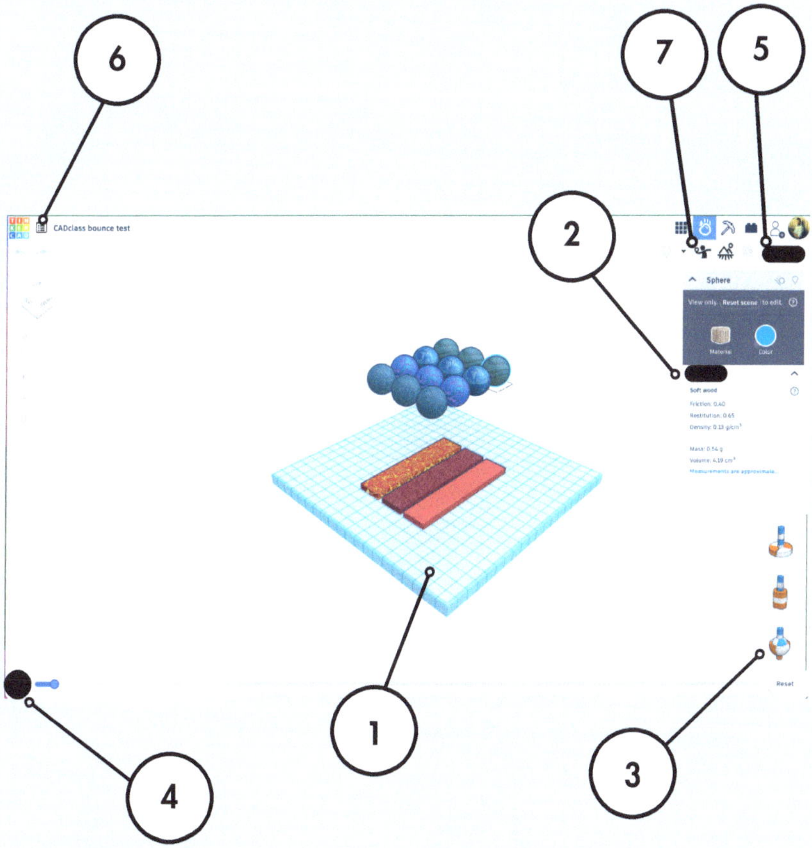

5. Share
6. Recent designs
7. Throwables

Solutions 

Simulation is a powerful feature in CAD because it allows designers and engineers to test and analyze their designs in a virtual environment before physically building them. Imagine you're designing a bridge for a river crossing project. With simulation, you can apply virtual forces and loads to see how the bridge behaves under different conditions, such as heavy traffic or strong winds. This helps you identify potential weaknesses or areas that need improvement. It's like playing a video game where you see the consequences of your design choices without any real-world risk.

Simulation in CAD also allows designers and engineers to explore how different materials and shapes affect the performance of their designs. For instance, if you're designing a chair, you can simulate the design to test its stability by applying gravitational forces. This way, you can make informed decisions about the design before investing time and resources in building a physical prototype. In essence, CAD simulation is like a digital playground where designers and engineers can experiment and learn from their mistakes without the time, cost, and environmental impact of using physical materials.

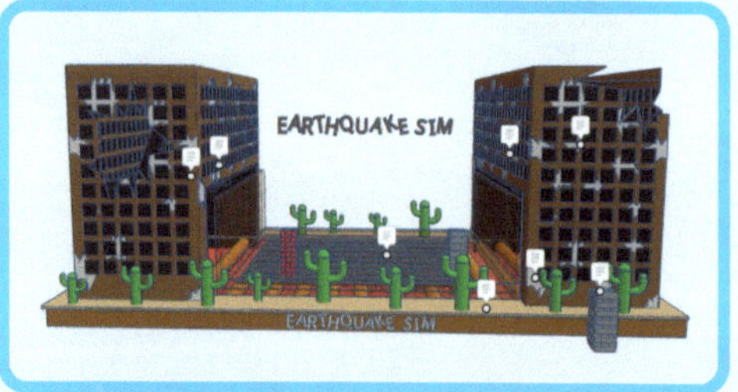

(Smoother) Sim Lab - Earthquake Simulator by SimulatedTinkering

t.ly/bdS6J

Ways you can use Sim Lab:

- Simulate gravity - place objects on slopes to see if they balance or tip over.
- Add materials - change material to see how the performance changes, e.g., does a steel wheel go faster than a rubber wheel?
- Throw stuff - simulate wind to see how designs respond to erratic loads.
- Build simple machines - experiment with materials and geometries.

Circuits

Now that you've explored 3D designs in Tinkercad, it's time to see what else is possible. Tinkercad Circuits is a virtual test lab for electronics like motors, lights, and sensors!

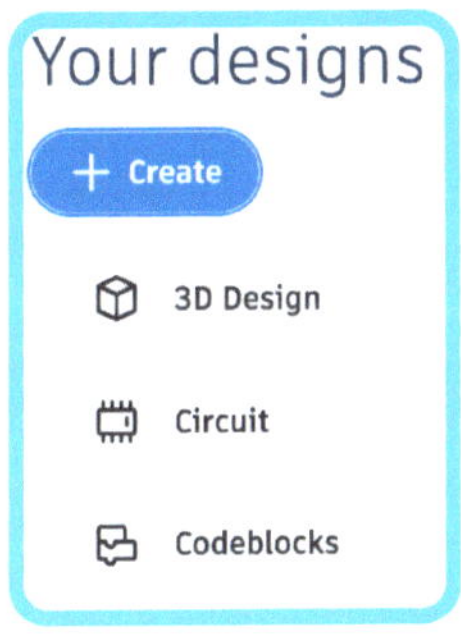

- Navigate to the dashboard.

- Press **+Create**.

- Press **Circuit** to open a new Circuit workspace.

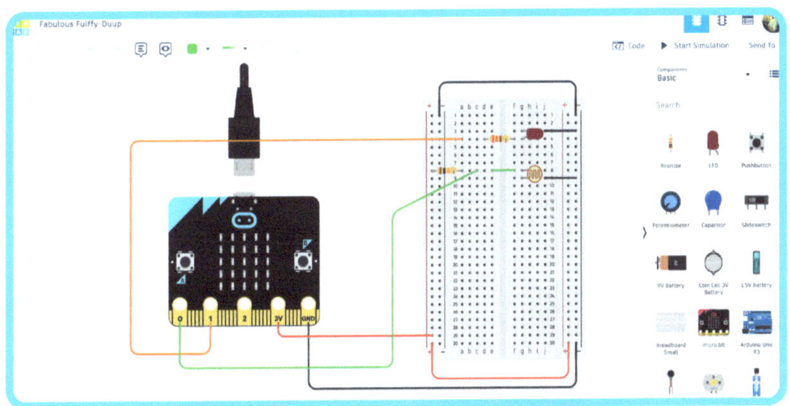

The **Circuits** workspace looks similar to the 3D workspace, with a searchable library on the right and buttons for different sub-workspaces on the top right.

Have a look around!

PLAY

Drag these components onto the workspace:
1. A resistor
2. An LED
3. A coin cell 3V battery
4. A slideswitch

Circuits 

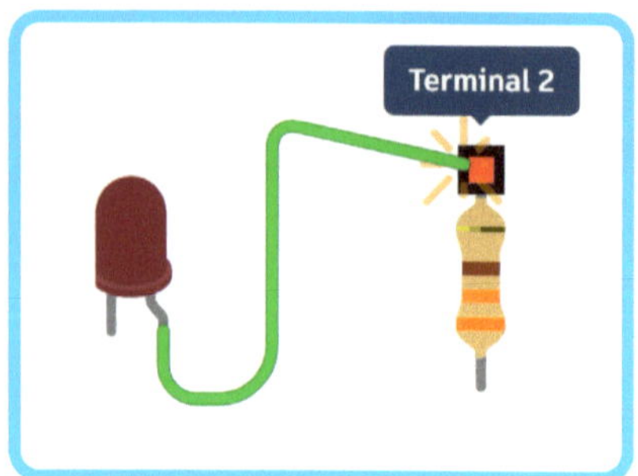

Click one of the legs of the LED. When you hover over it, it will tell you what it is.

Continue clicking to create a wire connection.

Join the wire to the top terminal of the resistor.

When it shows a red box, it's snapping to the end.

PLAY

Recreate this circuit.

Click on the resistor and use the Dialogue Box to change the value to 330 and the units from kΩ to Ω (kiloohms to ohms).

Notice how the color bands change.

Press the **Start Simulation** button, then press the switch to toggle it on/off.

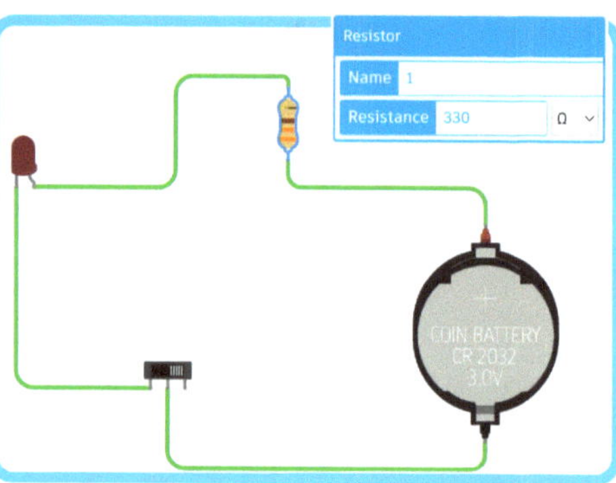

Remove the resistor and rewire the circuit. It exploded because there was too much current flowing into the LED, which wasn't protected by the resistor.

Circuits 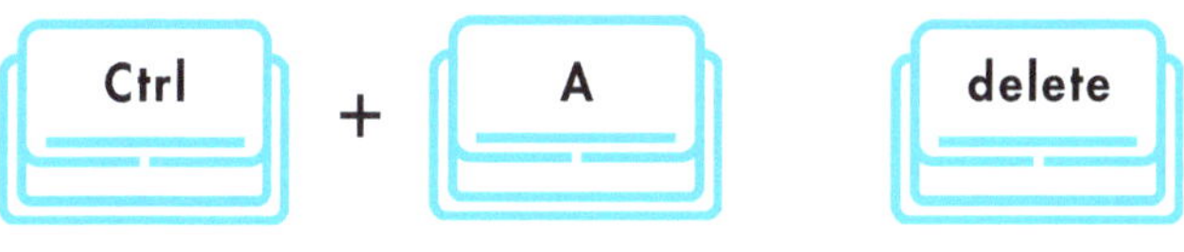

To clear the Circuits workspace, press Ctrl + A (select all) on your keyboard, then press delete.

Ctrl + **A**   **delete**

Navigate to these 2 buttons in the top right.

One will create a schematic of your circuit and the other will provide a bill-of-materials (a shopping list).

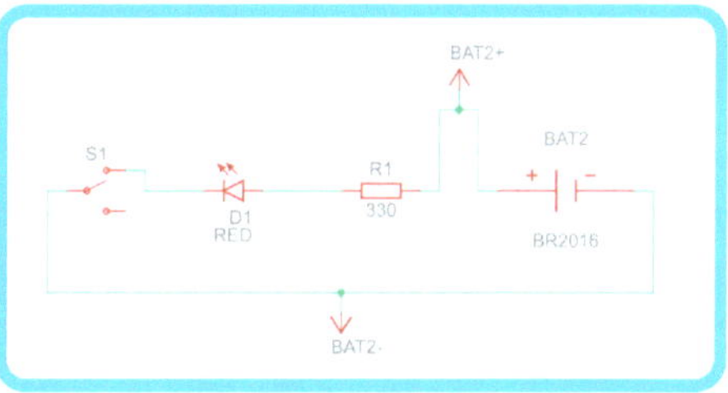

20

CHALLENGE

Create a circuit that turns a motor when near a light, using a photoresistor, a 9V battery and a hobby gear motor.

Circuits

With Tinkercad Circuits, you can drag electronic components such as resistors, capacitors, LEDs, microcontrollers, sensors, and more onto a virtual workspace. You can then connect these components using virtual wires to create circuits.

Once the circuit is designed, you can simulate its behavior in real-time. You can test how it performs under different conditions without needing physical components. This simulation capability is valuable for beginners learning about electronics and experienced engineers prototyping new designs.

Working with electronics at the component level involves several fundamental principles:

Component Identification: It is essential to identify different types of electronic components, such as resistors, capacitors, diodes, transistors, and integrated circuits. This includes recognizing their physical appearance, reading their markings, and understanding their specifications.

Understanding Component Characteristics: Each electronic component has specific electrical characteristics that determine its behavior in a circuit. This includes resistance, capacitance, voltage rating, current rating, frequency response, temperature coefficient, and more.

Circuit Analysis: Understanding basic circuit analysis techniques allows you to analyze circuits and predict their behavior. This includes Ohm's Law, Kirchhoff's Laws, voltage divider, and current divider laws.

Prototyping: Prototyping involves building circuits on a breadboard or in a digital environment like Tinkercad Circuits to test their functionality before finalizing a design. It allows for quick iteration and experimentation.

Troubleshooting: Troubleshooting skills are essential for identifying and fixing problems in electronic circuits. This involves systematic testing and measurement techniques to locate faults and determine the root cause of issues.

Search the gallery to find a vast array of pre-made Circuits.

Micro:bits

You can also use, code, simulate, and link-to Micro:bits! These are small digital programmable microprocessors (computers) that can be used to edit and control real-world objects using Scratch-style coding.

DO NOW

Go to the drop down menu in the top right corner and select Micro:Bit.

Select the Analogue starter and drag it on to the workspace.

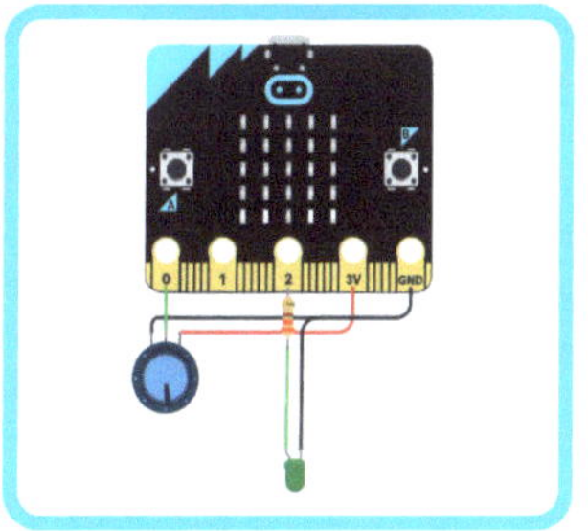

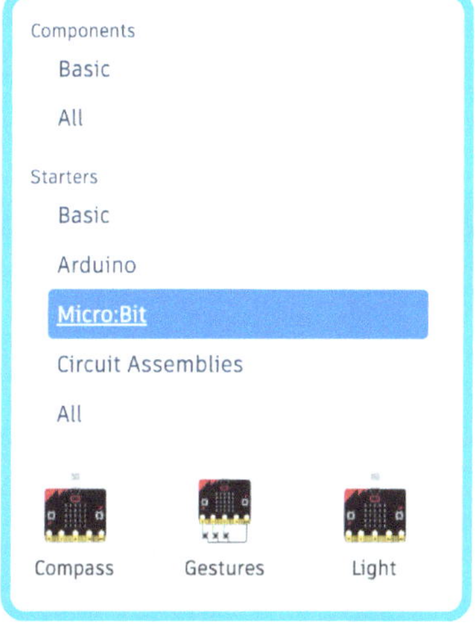

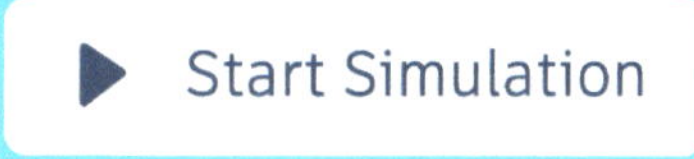

PLAY

Press the **Start Simulation** button then click and move to turn the Potentiometer dial in the bottom left.

This code creates a bar graph on the Micro:bit LED matrix and also lights up an external LED.

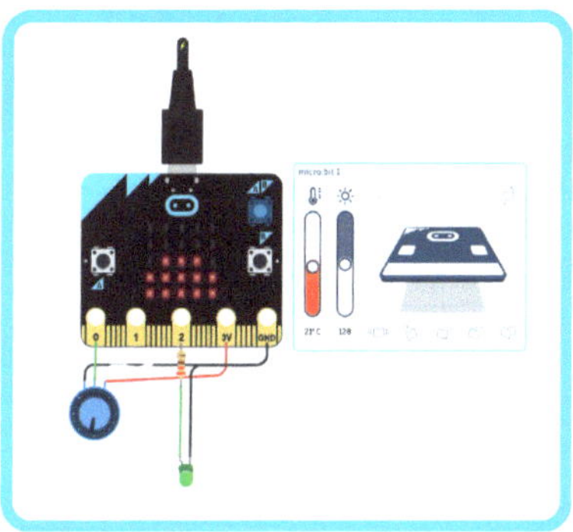

Micro:bits 

DO NOW

Press **Stop Simulation** and then press **Code** to expand the Coding area.

This is where you can program the Micro:Bit using blocks or text-based programming.

Minimize it by pressing the Code button again.

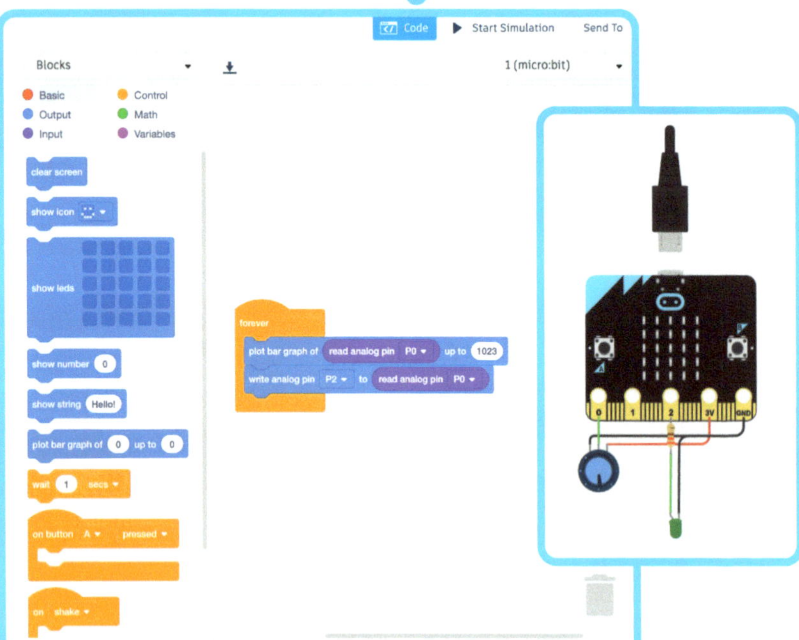

Micro:bits

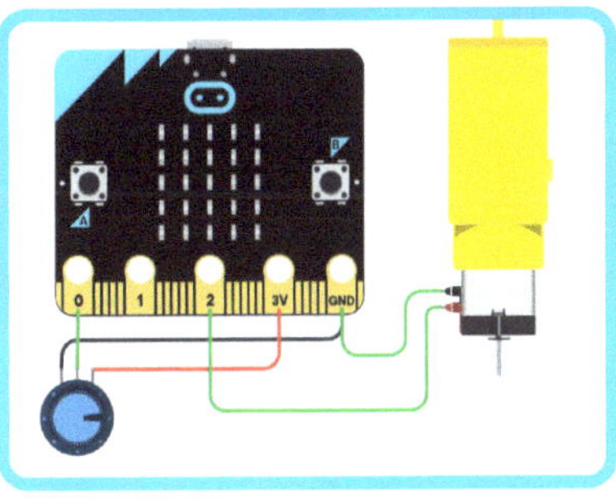

PLAY

Delete the LED and resistor and replace them with a HobbyGear motor.
Rewire it like in the image and re-start the simulation.

PLAY

If you want to learn more about Microbits go to tinkercad.com/learn and explore the **Circuits Micro:bits** tutorials.

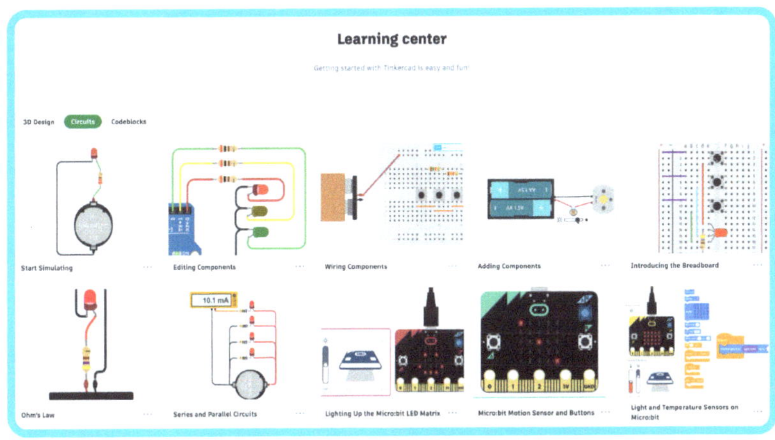

Save it
Name it "Micro:bit Motor"

Micro:bits 

Now that you've played around with circuits, it's time to introduce Micro:bits and Arduino.

Micro:bits are a small, programmable microcontroller board designed for education and learning purposes. The BBC developed it in partnership with several technology companies, including ARM, Microsoft, and the Python Software Foundation. The Micro:bit is a small, pocket-sized board with about 4 cm × 5 cm dimensions. It features several onboard sensors, including an accelerometer and a magnetometer, which allow it to detect motion and orientation. The Micro:bit has a 5x5 grid of LEDs that can be used to display text, numbers, and simple graphics. There are 2 programmable buttons on the Micro:bit that can be used as inputs for user interaction. The Micro:bit can be programmed using a variety of programming languages, including block-based languages like Microsoft MakeCode and Python.

Arduino is an open-source electronics platform based on easy-to-use hardware and software. It consists of a programmable circuit board (often called a microcontroller) and an Integrated Development Environment (IDE) used to write and upload computer code to the board. Arduino boards have inputs and outputs that allow them to interact with sensors, lights, motors, and other electronic components. The Arduino board is the physical hardware component of the platform. It typically contains a microcontroller chip, digital and analog input/output pins, a USB interface for programming and power, a voltage regulator, and other necessary components. Arduino IDE is the software used to write, compile, and upload code to the Arduino board. It's a simple yet powerful programming environment based on the C/C++ programming language. In Tinkercad Circuits, an Arduino can be programmed in Block Code or Text (C++).

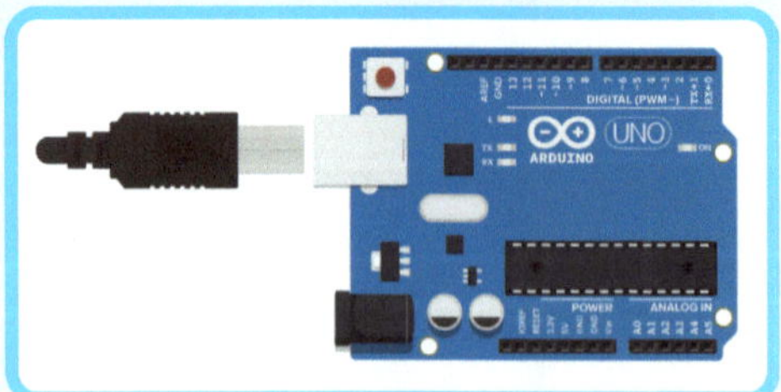

Micro:bits

The systems approach is a methodology that views complex phenomena as systems composed of interconnected and interdependent parts. This approach emphasizes understanding the relationships between these parts and how they function together. It's a helpful framework for thinking about electronic systems.

There are four fundamental concepts in the context of electronics using systems thinking. Take the example of a smoke alarm, like this one by Alekhine Samson Jr: t.ly/U7OKn

Input(s): Resources or information entering the system - power, CO_2, and heat levels.

Process: Activities or transformations occurring within the system - a circuit made of components or a microprocessor using coded software.

Output(s): Results or outcomes produced by the system - LEDs, speakers.

Feedback: Information generated by outputs, influencing future inputs or processes. The information that tells the alarm to sound or turn off.

If you want to learn more about Circuits, go to tinkercad.com/learn and explore the Circuits tutorials.

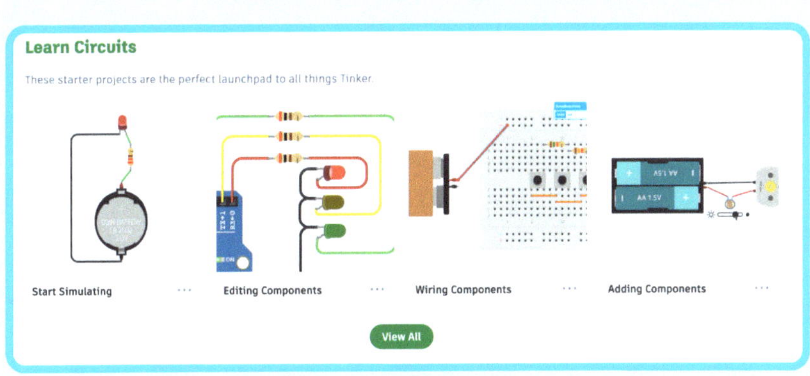

Codeblocks </>

Codeblocks is a tool for creating 3D designs using drag-and-drop sections of code. Instead of typing out complicated commands, you can snap together Scratch-style Codeblocks to create designs. It's a fun and easy way to simultaneously program and design in 3D.

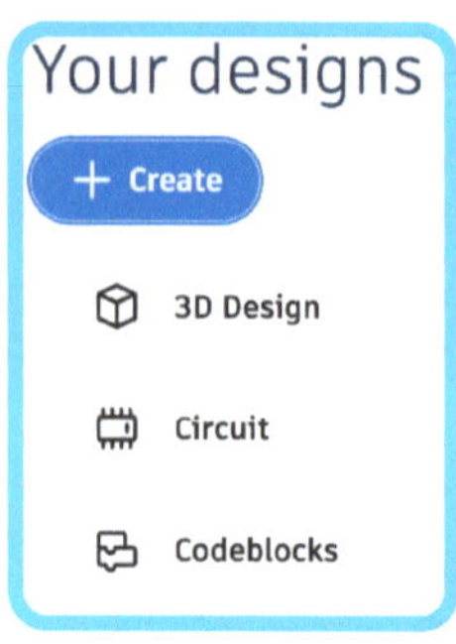

DO NOW

- Navigate to your dashboard page.

- Press **+Create.**

- Press **Codeblocks** to open a new Codeblock workspace.

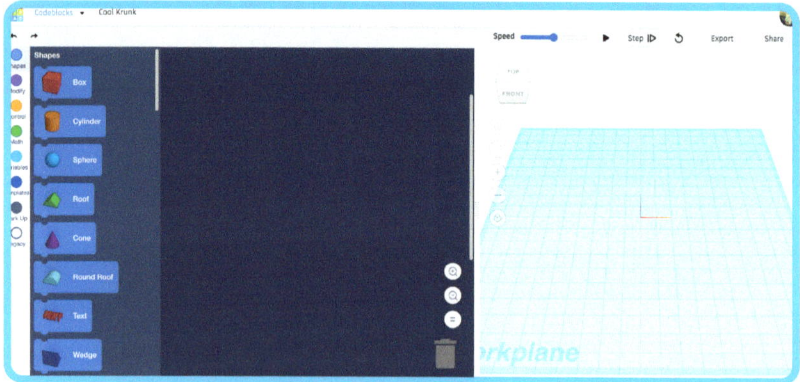

The **Codeblocks** workspace looks familiar, but it has a coding workspace on the left and a 3D workspace on the right. You can resize the sides by holding and sliding the middle vertical bar. Additional action buttons are in the top right.

Codeblocks </>

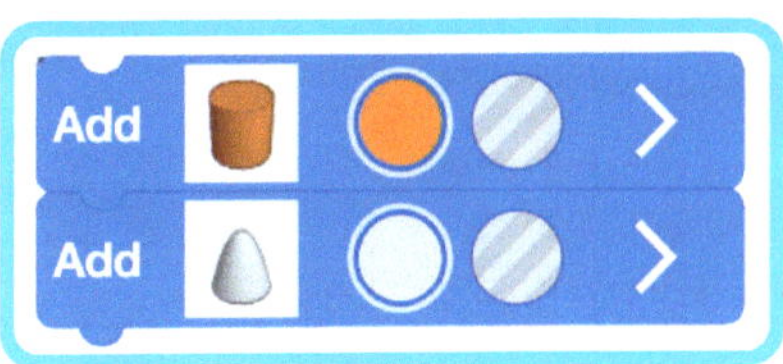

DO NOW

Drag in these shapes.

Press the **play** button in the top right.

Watch the code play and create.

Notice that the Paraboloid is hidden inside the Cylinder.

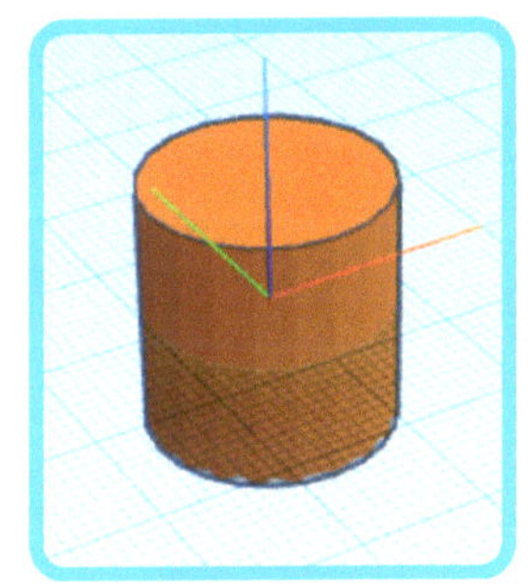

PLAY

Drag in these extra shapes then press the **play** button in the top right.

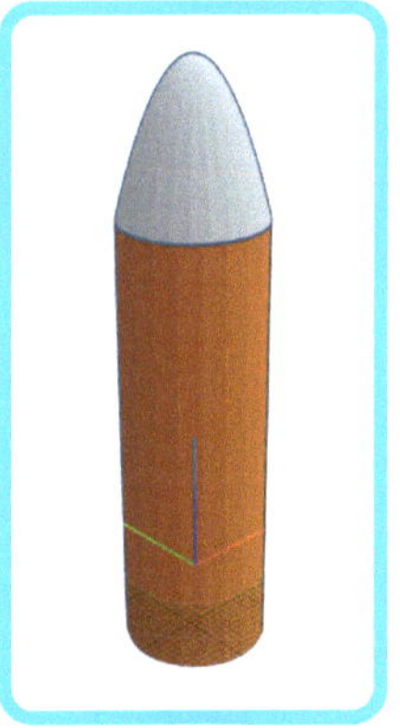

The purple block is modifying the previous shape. It sets the size and changes the location to the bottom center.

The second Move block shifts the Paraboloid to the top of the cylinder 60.0 mm up the Z axis.

Codeblocks </>

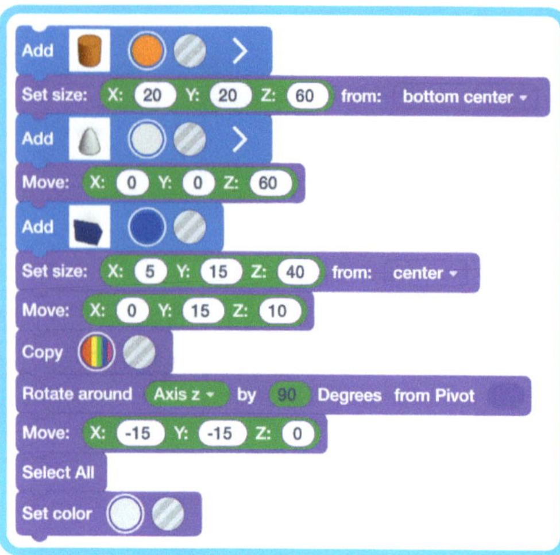

PLAY

Copy the rest of this code.

Then try to place the last 2 fins onto the base.

PLAY

To learn more about Codeblocks, visit tinkercad.com/learn and explore the Codeblocks tutorials.

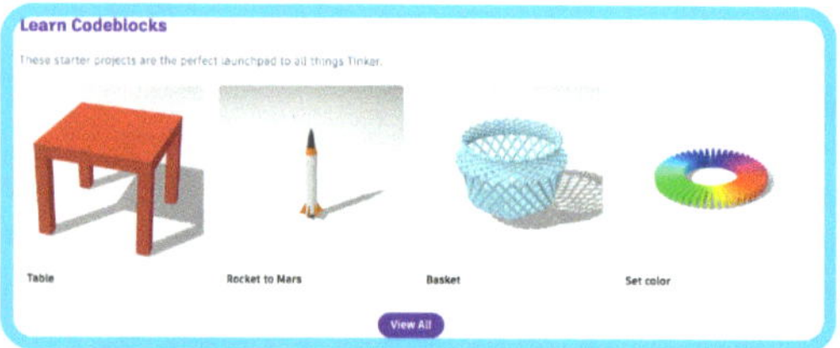

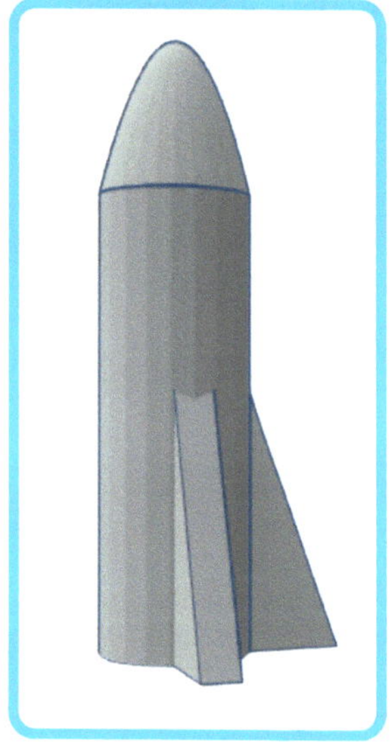

Save it
Name it "Codeblock Rocket"

Codeblocks 

Tinkercad Codeblocks is a programming environment designed for beginners, particularly aimed at introducing learners to coding concepts.

Tinkercad Codeblocks provides a visual programming interface where you can drag blocks representing different programming constructs, such as loops, conditionals, variables, and functions, to create programs. This visual approach allows you to understand coding logic without learning a specific programming language syntax.

With Tinkercad Codeblocks, you can create animations, interactive simulations, games, and other projects by assembling blocks logically. It's a user-friendly way to introduce coding concepts and foster creativity. Additionally, Tinkercad Codeblocks integrates with other features, allowing users to incorporate their code into 3D Designs via the Export button for a multidisciplinary learning experience.

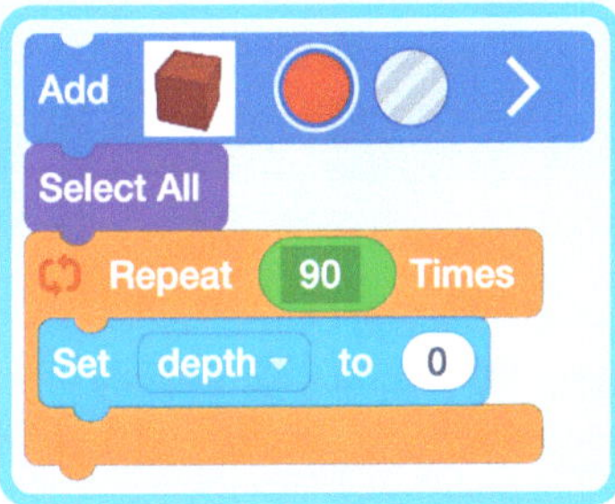

In Tinkercad Codeblocks, the main colored blocks represent different programming constructs or actions.

Red are for shapes, purple for modifiers, orange to control, green for maths, and Teal for Variables. Dark blue is for Templates, which creates reusable shapes.

If you want to learn more about Codeblocks go to tinkercad.com/learn and explore the Codeblocks tutorials.

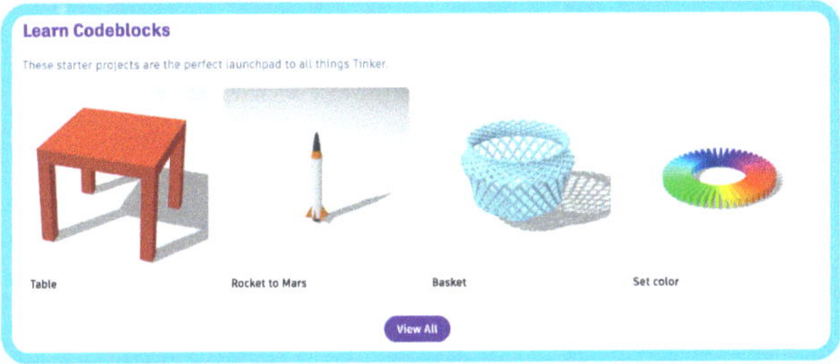

Design Challenges

21 CHALLENGE

Design a storage container or desk organizer.

22 CHALLENGE

Recreate your bedroom, adding dream features & furniture in 3D!

23 CHALLENGE

In Sim Lab create the longest Rube Goldberg machine / marble run you can!

24 CHALLENGE

Design a Mars Rover in 3D and use Circuits to prototype a sensor circuit!

Math Challenges

25 CHALLENGE

Design a measuring tool, for example, a scoop to measure 10g volumes.

26 CHALLENGE

Create designs using basic shapes, e.g., a robot with 4 Boxes, 2 Spheres, etc.

27 CHALLENGE

Use geometric measurement, e.g., rotate an object by 145 degrees.

28 CHALLENGE

Design & 3D print a Maths tool, for example, a 60-degree triangular ruler.

Science Challenges

CHALLENGE 29

Physics: Design and test a Rube Goldberg machine.

CHALLENGE 30

Biology: Create and label a cross-section of a cell.

CHALLENGE 31

Chemistry: Recreate a representation of a molecule e.g. caffeine.

CHALLENGE 32

Design & 3D print a tool to help with a science experiment e.g. a test tube rack.

Engineering

33 CHALLENGE

Design and 3D print an egg-drop holder to protect the egg cargo.

34 CHALLENGE

Reverse Engineer and recreate an existing design e.g. a clothes pin / peg.

35 CHALLENGE

Design a rubber band powered car or a Pinewood Derby car.

36 CHALLENGE

Design and prototype a tool to help with an engineering project e.g. a multi-tool for a bicycle or robot.

Electronics

Art Challenges

41 CHALLENGE

Create an ambigram tessellation like MC Escher.

42 CHALLENGE

Recreate famous artwork, like a geometric Mondrian abstract or famous architecture, like Big Ben.

43 CHALLENGE

Create a recurring pattern based on inspiration from nature, e.g. honeycomb.

44 CHALLENGE

Use the Scribble tool to create profile to duplicate around a point to create a vase.

Social Studies

45

CHALLENGE

Create a famous building like the Leaning Tower of Pisa, or Eiffel Tower.

46

CHALLENGE

Design an assistive device that helps someone with a specific need or disability e.g. arthritis.

47

CHALLENGE

Create a famous landmark or geographic feature e.g. a volcano or a drainage basin.

48

CHALLENGE

Recreate a Greek or Roman architectural feature, e.g. a Doric column.

End of Book Quiz

1. Name a specific piece of 'everyday' CAD software (not Tinkercad).

2. Give a unique advantage of CAD when compared to creating designs using "traditional" hand tools like pencils and paper.

3. Explain the disadvantages of using CAD vs. designing with pencil and paper.

4. Describe 2 ways CAD could contribute to cost or time savings in design and manufacturing.

5. Explain some limitations you came up against when using Tinkercad.

6. How might Augmented Reality (AR) help consumers understand a product?

7. Name some benefits of designers using CAD that allow for collaboration with other designers.

8. Name the parts of a piece of clothing Tinkercad is well suited to design in 3D. Why is this?

9. State specific examples of types of products that Tinkercad is not well suited to designing in 3D. Why is this?

10. Name industries where CAD is commonly used and explain how it benefits these sectors.

11. Describe the relationship between CAD and CAM.

12. Discuss the potential security concerns associated with CAD data.

13. Explain the Sim Lab as if you were talking to a 5-year-old.

14. Is copy & paste the same as duplicate? Explain your answer.

15. In what way can keyboard shortcuts help a CAD designer?

16. Think up a question for your teacher/instructor:

Solutions

1. Microsoft Word is a widely used desktop publishing software.

2. CAD allows for precise measurements and easy duplication of design features, which is hard to achieve with traditional hand tools.

3. A disadvantage of CAD is that it requires specialized software and skills, which can take time to acquire, especially for small-scale projects.

4. CAD can contribute to cost savings by reducing the need for physical prototypes and speeding up the design process, leading to faster time-to-market.

5. Some limitations of Tinkercad include its limited compatibility with other CAD software.

6. AR can help consumers understand a product by providing interactive 3D models and visualizations showing how the product works and can be used.

7. Some benefits of using CAD for collaboration include sharing and editing designs in real-time and communicating more effectively with team members.

8. Tinkercad is well suited for designing simple 3D shapes and structures, such as buttons and zippers because it has a user-friendly interface and essential modeling tools.

9. Tinkercad is not well suited for designing complex 3D shapes and structures, such as clothing patterns or detailed textures.

10. CAD is commonly used in aerospace, automotive, and manufacturing industries. It benefits these sectors by enabling faster and more accurate design iterations, reducing costs, and improving product quality.

11. CAD (Computer-Aided Design) is used to create digital models of products. In contrast, CAM (Computer-Aided Manufacturing) controls machines that produce physical prototypes or final products based on those models.

12. Some potential security concerns associated with CAD data include the risk of unauthorized access, theft, or modification of sensitive design information.

13. The Sim Lab is where you can learn how to use simulation software to test and improve designs before they're built in the real world. It's like a virtual playground where you can experiment with ideas and see how they work.

14. Copy and paste and duplicate are similar but different. Copy and paste creates a new copy of an object or text, while duplicate will paste selected objects and perform the previous action.

15. Keyboard shortcuts can help a CAD designer speed up everyday tasks, such as zooming in and out, rotating objects, or switching between different tools.

16 Q: "Can you recommend any resources or tutorials for learning more about CAD software and how to use it effectively?"

A: Yes, go to CADclass.org!

Add a Definition

Align ....

Group ....

Ungroup ....

Mirror ....

Viewcube ....

Scribble ....

Export ....

Import ....

Cruise ....

Add a Definition

Pan ....

Orbit ....

Zoom ....

Workplane ....

Copy ....

Paste ....

Duplicate ....

Move ....

Rotate ....

Shortcuts

View the workspace

+/-: zoom in/out

R: Ruler

P : pan

N: Notes

F: Fit selection

Middle mouse: pan

W: Workplane

Right mouse: Orbit

Commands

D: Drop to Workplane

Ctrl+D: Duplicate+repeat

Shift : select multiple

Ctrl+Z: Undo

Ctrl+C: Copy

Del: delete

Ctrl+V: Paste

Shortcuts

Functions

- : step move
- **Shift + Scale**: Uniform scale
- **Ctrl +** : Step move in Z
- **Alt + Scale**: Scale center
- **Shift +** : Step move
- **L**: Align
- **Shift + rotate:** 45° rotate
- **M**: Mirror

Shape properties

- **Ctrl+G**: Group
- **T**: Transparent
- **Ctrl+Shift+G**: ungroup
- **Ctrl+L**: Lock/unlock
- **H**: Hole
- **Ctrl+H**: Hide
- **S**: Solid
- **Ctrl+Shift+H**: Show all

Resources

We're committed to providing everyone with access to our books. Visit <u>CADclass.org/pages/books</u> for a free or donation-based copy of this book and others.

CADclass.org/courses/Tinkercad

YouTube.com/c/HLModTech

YouTube.com/@AutodeskTinkercad

Youtube.com/@robmorrill1

Instructables.com/Tinkercad

ESA.int/Education/Moon_Camp/Tinkercad

Weareprintlab.com/projects/designing-for-3d-printing

<u>Contact Information:</u>

Ed@CADclass.org

(415) 941 - 4114

About CADclass

CADclass is a platform for students and instructors to learn CAD, 3D printing, Design, and Engineering. We write books, teach online classes, and curate a worldwide community of makers. We provide free and paid resources through our social channels, website, and partner network.

Our book Mastering Fusion 360 is available on Amazon or for a donation/free on our website - CADclass.org/pages/books

Online Courses:

Tinkercad in Twenty Days - Step-by-step Tinkercad projects for advancing your Tinkercad skills beyond this book! CADclass.org/courses/tinkercad

3D Printing Masterclass - Ender3 Assembly and use for beginners! CADclass.org/courses/3dp

Mastering Fusion 360 - 28 step-by-step projects in Autodesk Fusion. CADclass.org/courses/CAD

Cura Masterclass - Turn your 3D models into 3D printable designs with Cura by Ultimaker! CADclass.org/courses/cura

Advanced 3D Printer Maintenance and Calibration - Fine-tune your 3D printer to get perfect prints every time! CADclass.org/courses/calibrate

Socials:

Youtube.com/@CADclassOfficial | Tiktok.com/@cadclass
Twitter.com/cad_class |
Instagram.com/cadclassofficial

CERTIFICATE

OF COMPLETION

Send an email to
Ed@CADclass.org with
"Certificate" in the title to receive a
digital certificate of completion!

Ed Charlwood

What's Next?

Make things. Take things apart. Fiddle with mechanical objects. Fix a broken tool. Take a woodworking, glassblowing, ceramic, or welding class. Visit your local library and get to know your librarian. Study a topic that interests you. Talk to an expert. Oil squeaky doors. Try to recreate objects you see. Curate a list of YouTubers who do amazing things. Study the great inventors. Visit an art gallery or museum. Start a business. Go deeper into 3D printing and laser cutting. Share what you know with someone else. Solve a problem you have in your own life. Start small, dream big, and keep going. Do what you've always wanted to do.

Life is short; don't waste any time!